A–Z

OF

GLOUCESTER

PLACES - PEOPLE - HISTORY

Roger Smith

AMBERLEY

Acknowledgements

No copyright material has been used in the preparation of this book. All photographs are the original work of the author. A thank you to my wife, Gillian, for taking second place to my computer while writing this book.

First published 2019

Amberley Publishing
The Hill, Stroud, Gloucestershire, GL5 4EP
www.amberley-books.com

Copyright © Roger Smith, 2019

The right of Roger Smith to be identified as the Author of this work has been asserted in accordance with the Copyrights, Designs and Patents Act 1988.

ISBN 978 1 4456 9199 2 (print)
ISBN 978 1 4456 9200 5 (ebook)

British Library Cataloguing in Publication Data. A catalogue record for this book is available from the British Library.

Typesetting by Aura Technology and Software Services, India. Printed in Great Britain.

Contents

Introduction

Gloucester is over 1,900 years old and was one of Roman Britain's most important towns. The cathedral is one of the finest in Britain, the place where William I decreed that the Domesday Book should be produced, where Edward II is buried and where Henry III was crowned. Its great east window is as large as a tennis court and was once the largest in the world. The historic docks is the most inland port in the country, from where ships used to sail to many European and North American ports, and where tall ships can still be seen today. Before the advent of motorways, all traffic from London to South Wales and from the north to the south-west of England had to pass over The Cross, which earned it the title of the crossroads of England. Behind modern shopfronts much of Gloucester's heritage can still be seen, including the UK's finest medieval merchant's house and a fifteenth-century coaching inn that, when built, was the country's largest. The Via Sacra provides a marked path around the centre following the line of the Roman city walls.

Sons of the city include Robert Raikes, a founder of the Sunday schools movement; George Whitefield, one of the founders of Methodism; and James 'Jemmy' Wood, once described as the richest commoner in England.

With that background, this book provides a fascinating insight into the city's historic streets, alleys and buildings, and some of its notable sons and daughters.

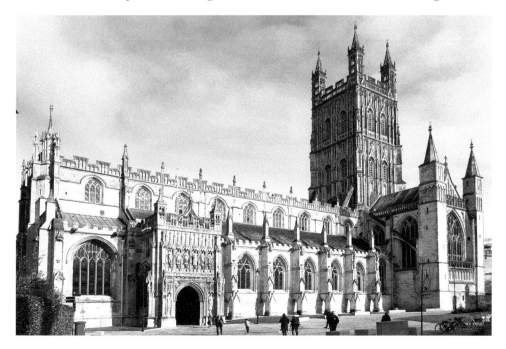

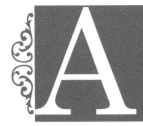

Æthelflæd

Æthelflæd (also spelt Ethelfleda) was the daughter of Alfred the Great and known as the Lady of the Mercians. In the late tenth century she and her husband Æthelred were rulers of Mercia. At that time Mercia's eastern territories were occupied by Danish Viking armies but, unlike the rest of England, much of English Mercia including Gloucestershire was unusually stable and Gloucester was important to Æthelflæd. In AD 900 she refortified the city and built a church, the New Minster, just outside the city walls; the Old Minster was St Peter's Abbey, now the cathedral. Although minster is sometimes referred to as a church, a minster was a settlement of clergy who lived a communal life and had an obligation to maintain the daily office of prayer. The ruins of the ancient wall near the junction of Priory Road and St Oswald's Road is the north wall of the New Minster, which is is Grade I listed.

In 909 Æthelflæd and her brother Edward, King of Wessex, successfully led an army into Danish-held Lincolnshire and brought back some powerful relics. Among these were the bones of St Oswald of Northumbria, which were placed in the crypt of the

St Oswald's Priory with the cathedral in the background.

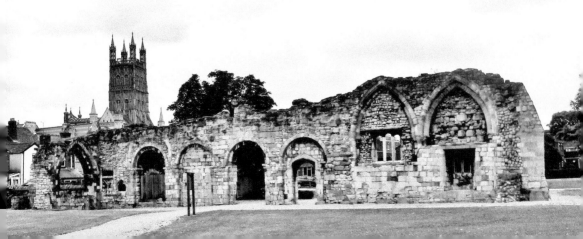

new church. After Æthelred's death he was also buried there. Æthelflæd continued campaigning against the Vikings until, by 918, she forced the Vikings to surrender their stronghold at York. She was on her way there when she died suddenly at Tamworth. Her body was then carried the 75 miles to Gloucester and she was buried alongside her husband. Her tombstone is now in the city museum.

For the next 100 years Æthelflæd's New Minster was famous for its wealth and miracles, and was nicknamed the Golden Minster. During the following century, however, St Oswald's fame and wealth declined until by 1100 the Old Minster, St Peter's Abbey, overshadowed S. Oswald's in every way. In 1152 St Oswald's became an Augustinian priory, which survived for nearly 400 years until 1537 when it was dissolved during the Dissolution of the Monasteries. Unlike most monasteries and priories St Oswald's had its own parishioners, so the arches were blocked up and the north aisle was converted into a little church. In 1656 this was pulled down, the only surviving part being the remains of the north wall shown in the photograph.

Alney Island

If you travel west from Gloucester by road or rail, very soon after leaving the city you must cross a causeway between what appears to be two large rivers. In fact, both are channels of the River Severn and the land between the two channels is Alney Island, a 3.5-km-long and 1.2-km-wide island, and nearly all of which is within the city boundaries. Until the Severn Bridge was built in 1966, Alney was the lowest point on the Severn where it could be crossed, and thus in medieval times it provided ideal protection from Welsh invaders.

Immediately after crossing Westgate Bridge by road, on the left is the Oxleaze where for many years the Three Counties Show was held when it was Gloucestershire's turn to be host. It was also where the city's annual Barton Fair was held and was the last of Gloucester's old charter fairs, with roots going back to a thirteenth-century royal charter. It was originally a cheese fair, sheep fair, hiring fair and pleasure fair but later became simply a funfair. To the right of the road is Pool Meadow, which houses the winter quarters for travelling show people.

The part of the island adjacent to the eastern channel of the Severn near Gloucester Docks is called Castlemeads, the name coming from the castle that for hundreds of years was directly opposite until it was demolished, and a prison was built in its place. In the Second World War an emergency power station was built here, but that has now been demolished.

At the western end is the hamlet of Over where three bridges – a rail, pedestrian, and road bridge – cross the river next to each other. The middle, pedestrian bridge was the original road bridge and was built by the Victorian engineer Thomas Telford in 1825 and remained in use until 1974. Although Over only has four letters, its pronunciation is the cause of much controversy as many people pronounce it 'oover', as in Hoover, while others pronounce it as in 'over there'.

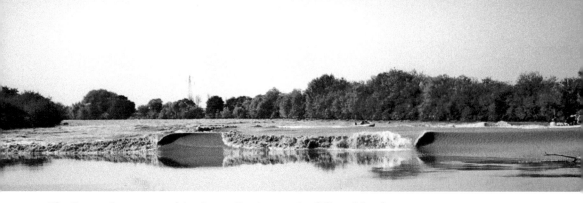

The Severn Bore approaching Lower Parting south of Alney Island.

Alney Island regularly witnesses one of Britain's great natural wonders – the Severn Bore. The River Severn has the third highest tidal range in the world, and incoming tides combined with the river's funnel-shaped estuary causes the front of the oncoming surge of water to create a great wave. Bores occur twice a day on about 130 days a year, on the days immediately following the new and full moon. An ideal site to view the bore is from Telford's bridge at Over.

B

Baker's Clock

In Southgate Street a few metres from The Cross is the beautifully preserved Edwardian shopfront of G. A. Baker & Son, jewellers. Outside the shop is Gloucester's most recognisable public clock, below which is Father Time holding a scythe flanked by figures representing people from each country of the British Isles: Miss Ireland

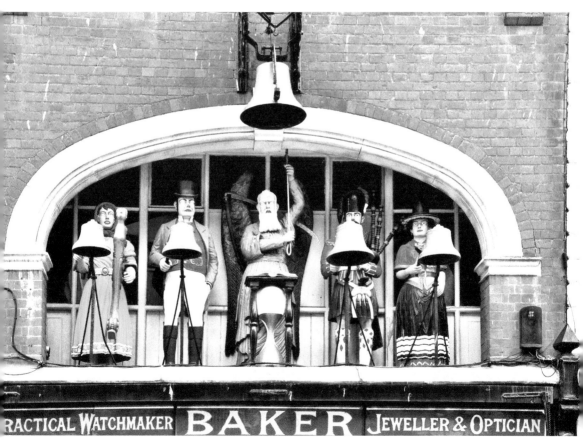

RACTICAL WATCHMAKER · BAKER · JEWELLER & OPTICIAN

Baker's clock with Father Time and figures representing Ireland, England, Scotland and Wales.

with a harp, John Bull from England, a Scottish piper and Miss Wales. Father Time strikes the large bell every hour while the other figures chime their smaller bells every quarter of an hour. The figures are the work of local craftsmen who carved figureheads for sailing ships.

St Bartholomew's Hospital

During medieval times there were at least three hospitals in the city: St Mary Magdalene's, the Hospital of St Margaret and St Sepulchre, and St Bartholomew's, which was the largest and wealthiest of the three. The first buildings here date from Henry II's reign when the Westgate Bridge was being built. They provided shelter for the bridge builders as well as for sick men and women from the surrounding area.

In 1528 the hospital was rebuilt on higher foundations to raise it above flood level. Elizabeth I granted it her patronage in 1564 and directed that it was to maintain a priest, physician, surgeon and forty alms people. It was also to be named the Hospital of St Bartholomew of the foundation of Queen Elizabeth. Upon the death of the incumbent governor, the hospital's ownership reverted to the city corporation in 1566 who found the buildings to be in a terrible state. The city corporation then rebuilt nineteen of the alms peoples' rooms and made considerable improvements to other parts of the building. The hospital was completely rebuilt to its current design in the late eighteenth century.

In 1890 St Bartholomew's merged with St Margaret's, St Magdalene's and a now-demolished St Kyneburgh's Hospital to form the United Hospitals with the new title Gloucester Municipal Charities, although the old St Bartholomew's building remained in use. Today, St Bartholomew's houses a business centre and retail outlets.

St Bartholomew's Hospital seen from Westgate Street.

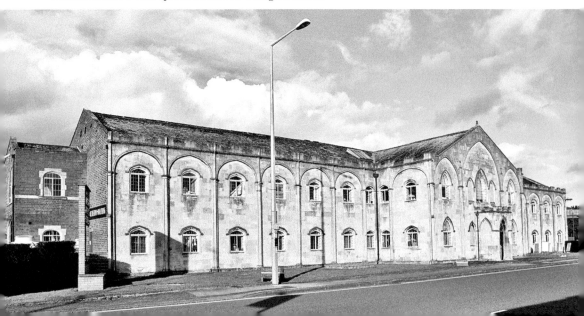

Barton Street

Effectively an extension of Eastgate Street, the Barton Street area is possibly the most multicultural street in Britain, with six churches and residents from at least twenty-five countries. Settlement in the area dates back to the thirteenth century. From the late eighteenth until the early twentieth century there were a number of watermills in the area alongside the River Twyver, and both Mill Street and Millbrook Street provide reminders of their existence. In 1873 an outdoor swimming pool was built next to the Twyver near where it passes under Millbrook Street.

In the early nineteenth century ornamental gardens including a bowling green and tea garden were laid out near Vauxhall Road. At the same time there was also an ironworks near here.

The city's horse tramways opened in 1879 with one of the main routes along Barton Street. The depot was in India Road, but in 1904 the tramways were converted to run on electricity and a new depot was built in Bristol Road. The India Road site was then converted into a roller skating rink.

On the corner of Blenheim Road a cinema opened in 1923. Originally called the Picturedrome, it closed in 1962, having been renamed The Ritz. It reopened as a bingo hall but closed once more in 1984. The Gloucester Operatic and Dramatic Society then bought it, enlarged the stage and reopened it in 1986 as the New Olympus Theatre. The auditorium is notable for its exceptionally rich plasterwork to the walls, ceiling and balcony front.

For many years the area had a large number of public houses, most of which opened in the mid to late nineteenth century. The only one now open is One Eyed Jacks, which opened in 1847 as the Victoria House Inn. Worthy of mention is the now-closed Robin Hood Inn in Hopewell Street. The ground floor at the front is covered with green glazed tiles, while above the front door is a carved stone panel that reads 'Ye Olde Robin Hood Inn'.

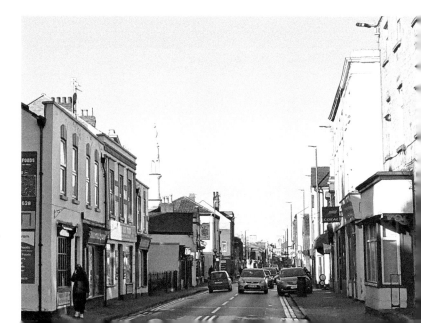

Barton Street with the minaret of Jamia al Karim Mosque prominent.

Bell, Sir Thomas

Although Sir Thomas Bell was three times mayor of Gloucester and four times its MP, he is largely unknown by most Gloucester residents. He was one of the city's largest employers, one of its wealthiest citizens, a philanthropist, and also became the city's largest private landowner.

Following the Dissolution of the Monasteries, in 1539 Bell and his wife purchased Blackfriars Priory and turned its cloister and scriptorium into a cap factory employing 300 people. Income from that trade which made him Gloucester's wealthiest citizen. He also converted the priory's church into a grand mansion that he referred to as 'My howse called Bell Place'.

A few years after opening his cap factory, again benefiting from the Dissolution of the Monasteries, Bell founded Kimbrose Hospital in Southgate Street near the present Kimbrose Triangle. The name Kimbrose was derived from St Kyneburgh's Chapel as the hospital was built on the site of the chapel, which, together with an adjoining cottage, he had bought from the Crown.

Bell's wife, Lady Bell, always seemed to use a particular gate as her entrance into the priory. This eventually became known as Lady Bell's Gate, which gave rise to the name Ladybellegate Street for the adjacent street. Bell and his wife are both buried in St Mary de Crypt Church.

Sir Thomas Bell's mansion at Blackfriars Priory.

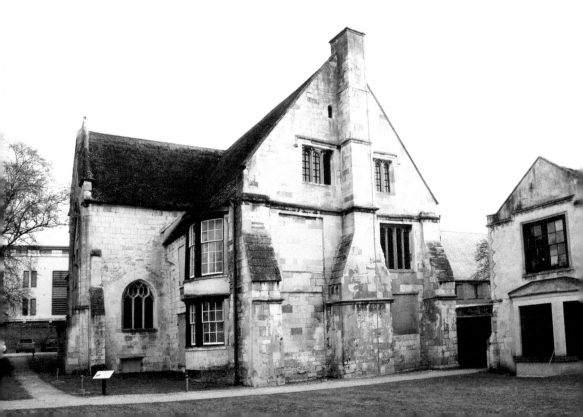

Blackfriars

Blackfriars Priory is the most complete example of a medieval Dominican priory in Britain and is Grade I listed. The cloister is original and includes the scriptorium where friars were trained for their preaching mission over 750 years ago. The friars' study cells were known as carrels, and twenty-nine of them still exist in England's oldest surviving library building. During Henry VIII's Dissolution of the Monasteries, to save the library's books from being destroyed many of them were taken to Edinburgh, since at that time it was outside Henry's jurisdiction.

Blackfriars was named after the black cloaks that its friars wore. It was built in the bailey of Gloucester's Norman castle, with funds provided by Henry III, who was crowned in Gloucester Cathedral. The friary originally resembled a small monastery with buildings arranged around a cloister, which included a church, chapter house, library, buttery, refectory, dormitory and infirmary. Next to the buttery was a small room that had a door to a path leading down to the River Severn. An on-site brewery provided the friars with ale and there was a guesthouse for visitors in nearby Ladybellegate Street.

Henry VIII seized the friary during his Dissolution of the Monasteries and sold it to Sir Thomas Bell, who converted it into a cap factory. In the 1930s part of the friary was divided into two separate houses with the rest being taken over by a drinks company and a printers. They closed in 1960 and English Heritage took over the building and restored it.

The south range of Blackfriars Priory.

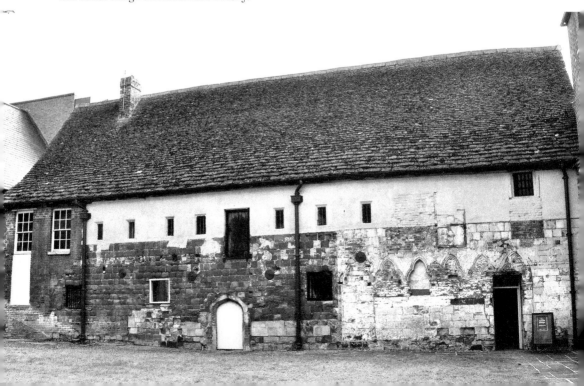

Bull Lane

Bull Lane is Gloucester's narrowest street. It runs between Westgate Street and Longsmith Street, although there is no longer any vehicle access at the Westgate Street end. The lane dates from around 1260 and was originally called Gore Lane because of the large number of pig sties and slaughter houses in the area.

In 1708 The Bull Inn opened in the lane, which was accordingly renamed Bull Lane, although there had been an inn in the lane since at least 1682. The Bull Inn closed in 1910 and for a time it was used as an antiques warehouse, but that was later demolished to make way for an extension to the city's telephone exchange.

For many years afterwards the lane had no businesses of note until Peppers Café opened in 2011. As can be seen in the photograph the outside of the café is decorated with a fine selection of street art. In 2016 Angie's Bar opened as Gloucester's smallest pub, which is appropriate given its location in the city's narrowest street. In the pavement at the Westgate Street end is a mosaic depicting the bull after which the lane is named.

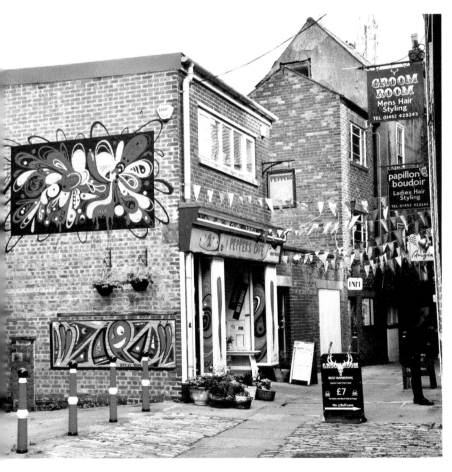

Bull Lane looking towards Westgate Street.

C

Café René

Tucked away down an alley called Marylone off Southgate Street you will find one of Gloucester's best-kept secrets, a French-style restaurant, café and bar called Café René. The café's cellars were previously used as wine vaults, and at one time both spirits and beer were brewed here.

In the bar are two medieval wells around 20 metres apart, although only one is visible. One is a soft water well that may have been used by Franciscan friars from the nearby Greyfriars monastery to make spirits, the other was used for soft drinks and possibly beer. During the Gloucestershire floods in July 2007 Gloucester's mains water supply was cut off due to contamination at the Mythe waterworks near Tewkesbury, and the wells provided the café with its very own water supply.

This is a medieval building that is reputed to have six ghosts and a poltergeist as permanent residents. Among the ghosts said to frequent the bar are a twelfth-century

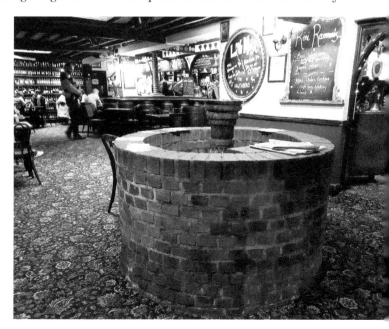

Medieval well in the bar at Café René.

monk who roams around with a candle, an elderly woman, a ginger-bearded middle-aged man, and a poltergeist that has been known to pour itself spirits from the optics, smash glasses and throw packets of crisps around. When the landlord was packing up the till takings one night after everyone had left, he felt a hand on him and dropped the takings in fright, but when he went back the next day the money was still there. Apparently, ghosts don't need money.

Cathedral

Gloucester's greatest treasure is its cathedral, one of Britain's most beautiful and considered one of the seven most beautiful cathedrals in the world. The building has Romanesque and Perpendicular styles that are of outstanding interest and importance, and most great English cathedrals can trace part of their design to innovations that were developed here, including the breathtaking fan vaulting at King's College Chapel in Cambridge, the complex lierne vaulting in the cloisters at Canterbury, and the Perpendicular technique of the cloisters at Westminster Abbey.

Founded in AD 681 as the Abbey of St Peter by Oscric, a ruler of the Hwicce tribe, it was rebuilt on a grander scale in 1058. When William I faced an invasion from Canute IV of Scandinavia in 1085, he moved his court to Gloucester and while here he initiated the production of the Domesday Book.

The abbey was destroyed by fire in 1088. Construction of a new building began soon after and this was consecrated in 1100. Just twenty-two years later another fire ripped through the abbey, but this time structural repairs were delayed because the monastery was in financial trouble. The monks were forced to sell their silver as part of a ransom for Richard I in 1194, then thirteen years later King John seized one third of their property. However, rebuilding of the abbey had continued and in 1216 it was far enough advanced to hold the coronation of the nine-year-old Henry III. A great deal of that church survives including the entire crypt, much of the east end, the great piers in the nave, most of the north aisle and the Norman Chapter House. Richard II held his Parliament here in 1378.

Not to be missed are the cloisters that are notable for their magnificent fan vaulting, the technique being invented here in the 1350s. Also in 1350 the great east window was installed. It is as big as a tennis court, was once the largest window in Europe, and fills the entire east end of the building. The window commemorates the Battle of Crécy and the siege of Calais, and is considered to be England's first war memorial. Another stained-glass window dating back to 1350 features one of the earliest images of golf, and is over 300 years older than the next earliest image of golf recorded in Scotland.

The cathedral became a popular pilgrimage destination as besides abbots and other ecclesiastical officials buried here, it is the burial place of William the Conqueror's eldest son, Robert Curthose, Duke of Normandy, and Edward II, whose shrine was a significant source of revenue; the decorative cage that encloses his effigy is one of the

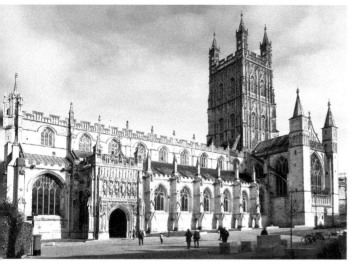

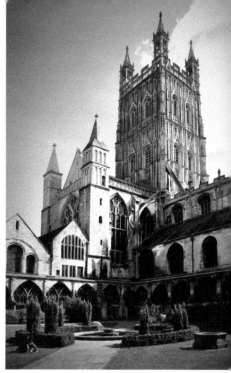

Above: Gloucester Cathedral seen from College Green.

Right: Gloucester Cathedral's tower and the cloister garden.

earliest alabaster carvings in England. Also buried here is John Stafford Smith, who composed the music for the American national anthem *The Star Spangled Banner*.

In 1536 Parliament passed an act dissolving all monasteries with incomes under £200 per year, leading to St Peter's Abbey being officially closed on 2 January 1540. However, the original abbey building was spared from destruction because of its connection to the monarchy. Henry VIII intended to create twenty-one new dioceses and bishoprics, and Gloucester was one of six that was actually preserved. In September 1541 it was made the Cathedral Church of the Holy and Invisible Trinity in the newly created diocese of Gloucester.

The cathedral features as a location in many films: the cloisters were transformed into the corridors of Hogwarts for *Harry Potter and the Philosopher's Stone*, *The Chamber of Secrets* and *The Half Blood Prince*; it was also used as the setting for the 2008 *Doctor Who* Christmas special; parts of BBC's Shakespeare series *The Hollow Crown*; Damian Lewis's *Wolf Hall*; and *Sherlock* starring Benedict Cumberbatch and Martin Freeman.

Christ Church

In 1814 some mineral springs were discovered at the end of Brunswick Road, and a spa was opened to capitalise on them. To cater for the needs of the growing number of people moving into the area, a church was opened in 1822, the cost of construction having been met by the local residents. It was originally known as the Spa Church but after a few years the spa waters failed and so did the church. It was then taken over by the diocese of Gloucester in the 1850s and renamed Christ Church. The west front was subsequently rebuilt in an Italian Romanesque style.

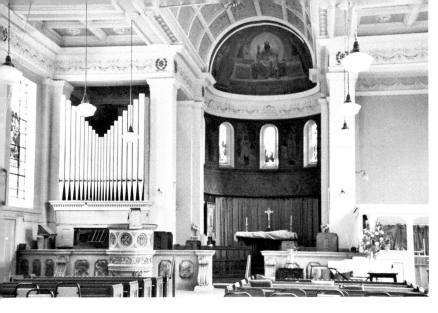

The art nouveau interior of Christ Church.

The interior has been described as a little gem. The ceiling has a central barrel vault that terminates in a semi-dome within an art nouveau-style apse, and a flat ceiling on either side. The apse is decorated with a mural of angels in art nouveau style and has three windows fitted with memorial glass. One of the stained-glass windows has a portion of clear glass, the result of shrapnel damage sustained during the Second World War.

College Court

Unlike many streets in Gloucester that have suffered in the name of progress, College Court has survived virtually unscathed. Running from Westgate Street through St Michael's Gate to the cathedral precincts, it is one of Gloucester's few remaining medieval pedestrian alleys and certainly its best preserved. It dates from at least 1333 when it was named Craft's Lane, then went through various name changes including Ironmonger's Row and St Peter's Lane until finally becoming College Court in 1778.

In 1413 four tenements were built on the west side of the lane, but these were replaced in the eighteenth century by the terrace that is there today, although parts of the terrace may incorporate remnants from the fifteenth to seventeenth centuries.

The most significant building in the alley is No. 9, which was substantially remodelled in 1979 to become The World of Beatrix Potter for the publisher F. Warne. The alterations were designed to replicate illustrations of the tailor's shop in Beatrix Potter's story *The Tailor of Gloucester*; the actual tailor's shop was in The Sword Inn in Westgate Street.

At the end of College Court is a fourteenth-century archway, St Michael's Gate, which started life as a pedestrian gateway in the precinct wall of St Peter's Abbey. The gateway was the entrance to the abbey's cemetery, and was also used by pilgrims visiting the shrine of Edward II.

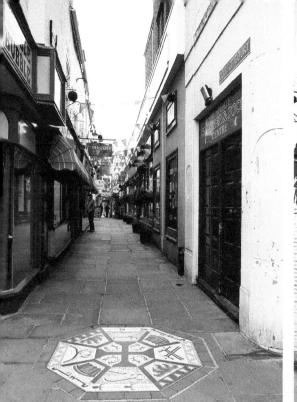

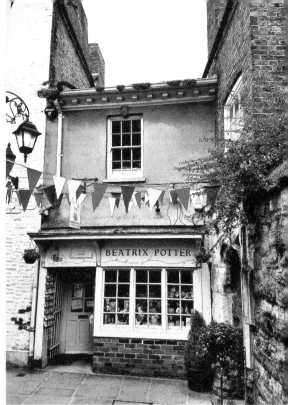

Above left: College Court seen from Westgate Street.

Above right: The house of The World of Beatrix Potter in College Court.

Right: St Michael's Gate seen from College Court.

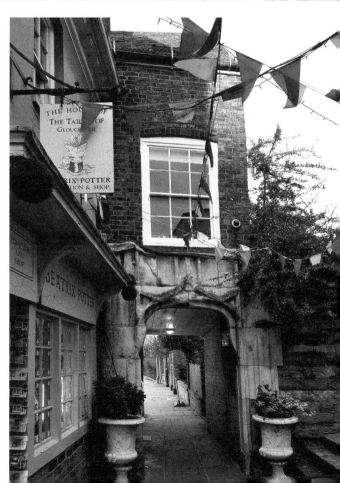

College Green

College Green is a well-proportioned close surrounding the south and west side of the cathedral. Most of the buildings date from the seventeenth and eighteenth centuries. On the west side of the green, four of the houses were built on the site of the stables and coach houses of the bishop and dean, while No. 12 includes a ground-floor assembly room that at one time was used for concerts and social gatherings.

At the west end of the green are two Grade I listed gateways: the Inner Gate adjoining No. 15 goes through to Millers Green, while St Mary's Gate dates from the fourteenth century and provides access to St Mary's Square. The house adjoining St Mary's Gate incorporates substantial remains of a monastic building, possibly from the almonry of St Peter's Abbey.

At the west end of the green is a First World War memorial to the Royal Gloucestershire Hussars Yeomanry. This was unveiled in 1922 and is adorned with bronze bas-relief panels depicting episodes from the regiment's campaigns in Egypt, Gallipoli, Sinai, Palestine and Syria. After the Second World War another relief panel was added to the memorial.

More recently, the area at the east end of the green has been landscaped with funding provided by the Heritage Lottery Fund to allow the cathedral to achieve its mission of being 'In tune with heaven, in touch with daily life'. This area was originally the lay cemetery for St Peter's Abbey.

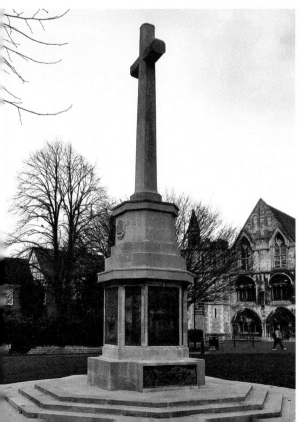

Memorial to the Royal Gloucestershire Hussars in College Green.

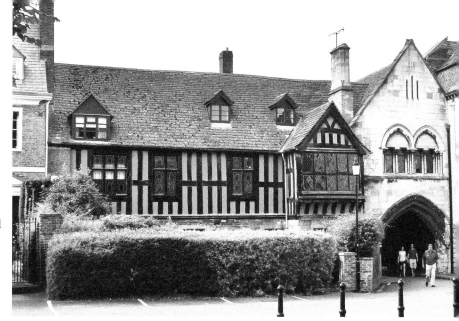

Grade I listed St Mary's Gate and the Almoner's Lodging in College Green.

College Street

College Street has always provided the main access from Westgate Street to the cathedral. It dates from at least 1139 when it was named Lychlone, the word 'lych' meaning a 'roofed gateway to a churchyard', which was appropriate as it ran from opposite the porch of the former Holy Trinity Church in Westgate Street to King Edward's Gate at the entrance to the cathedral precincts. Since then the street has undergone various name changes including Abbey Lane, St Edward's Lane and Lower College Lane, finally becoming College Street in 1780.

King Edward's Gate is on the site of an earlier gatehouse that was demolished in the seventeenth century to create a wider entrance to the cathedral. The earlier gatehouse was where the abbot of St Peter's Abbey received the body of Edward II for burial following his death at Berkeley Castle in 1327.

In 1890 the buildings on the east side of the street were demolished and the street widened. Buildings on the west side were unaltered and include probably the most photographed subject in the city after the cathedral – a row of fifteenth-century half-timbered buildings, one of which is a cosy little café aptly named The Comfy Pew.

On the east side a terrace of five shops and offices accentuate the street's importance as the approach to the cathedral. Also on this side is a gateway leading to an alley that was formerly called King Edward's Lane. A room above the gateway forms a bridge between the terraced shops and a building on the corner of College Green. Another building at the end of the alley links with three Italianate-style buildings in Westgate Street.

To commemorate the cathedral's 900th anniversary, in 1992 a pair of ornate gates were erected next to King Edward's Gate. Moulded into the top of each gate pillar are shields bearing crossed keys that represent St Peter, in recognition that until 1541 the cathedral was known as St Peter's Abbey.

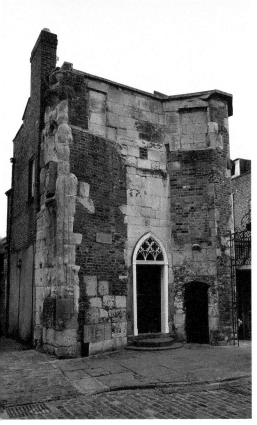

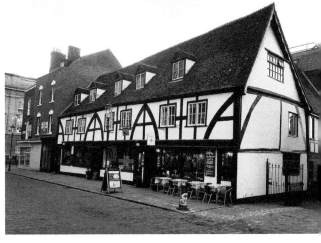

Above: The Comfy Pew restaurant in College Street.

Left: King Edward's Gate at the end of College Street.

Below: Entrance to College Street from Westgate Street.

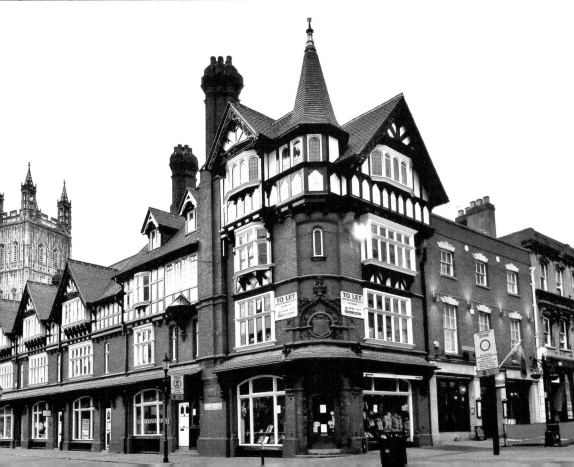

Cross Keys Lane

If you walk down Southgate Street from The Cross, after about 80 metres you will come to Cross Keys Lane. It was originally called Scroddelone, 'scrodde' being an Anglo-Saxon word for a shroud or garment reflecting the fact that in the tenth century it was the centre of the city's cloth trade; a mosaic plaque commemorating the trade is set into the pavement at the end of the lane.

The lane runs from Southgate Street to Bull Lane, and halfway along is the very narrow Mercer's Entry, also known as Pinch Belly Alley, on the corner of which is Mercers Hall. That was built in the eighteenth century as a warehouse and store, and was later occupied by a local cider merchant and brewer who used the upper floor as a granary. Since 1955 it has been occupied by the Gloucester Freemasons; the former granary is now the Masonic temple.

Since 1780 the lane has been named after its most prominent building, the Cross Keys Inn, a Grade II listed timber-framed building that was originally three cottages. It has been an inn since at least 1720, but the name suggests possible older origins as prior to the Reformation the sign of crossed keys meant that the inn was supplied with beer and wine by a nearby monastic house. Crossed keys is also the emblem of St Peter to whom the abbey, now the cathedral, was dedicated. In the nineteenth century the inn used to have its own brewhouse, but around 1894 it was tied to the City Brewery.

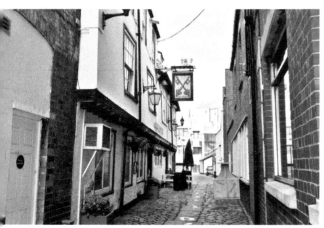

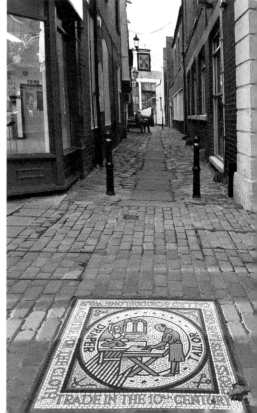

Above: Cross Keys Inn in the very narrow Cross Keys Lane.

Right: Cross Keys Lane seen from Southgate Street.

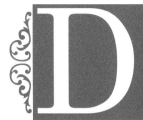

Docks

Gloucester was granted port status in 1580 by Elizabeth I and is the UK's most inland port. However, the tidal stretch of the River Severn approaching the city is very narrow and caused difficulties in navigation so few foreign-going vessels ventured this far up the river. In 1827 the Gloucester & Sharpness Canal opened, which allowed ships to bypass the difficult stretch of river and heralded the sight of foreign ships moored in the docks. When the canal was first opened it was the widest and deepest

The National Waterways Museum at Gloucester Docks.

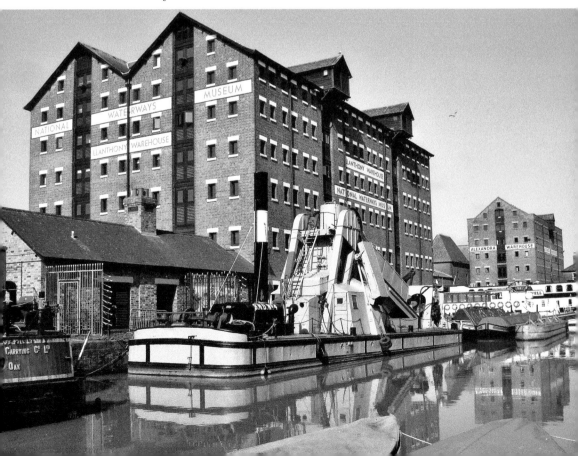

in England. Here large sea-going ships offloaded their cargoes so they could be transported by barge on the River Severn up to the Midlands; corn came from Ireland and Europe, sugar from the Caribbean and timber from Scandinavia, while salt came from Worcestershire to be exported.

Fifteen fine Victorian warehouses still stand as reminders of the past. They were built between 1827 and 1873 for storing salt and corn, but now they are used as offices, housing and shops, and in the case of Llanthony Warehouse, as the home of the Waterways Museum, which portrays life on the waterways between the Bristol Channel and the Midlands and has a number of historic craft on display. Where ships once discharged their cargoes, now there is an ever-changing miscellany of narrowboats, smart motor cruisers, yachts and tall ships. There is also a range of waterfront bars, restaurants and coffee shops.

The docks regularly hosts a tall ships festival, when the main basin with its warehouses resembles a scene from the 1800s. The old warehouses have also provided ideal backgrounds for shooting scenes for feature films such as *Alice Through the Looking Glass* starring Johnny Depp and many period television dramas such as *The Colour of Magic* starring David Jason.

Two dry docks are still fully operational. Here wooden sailing ships can often be seen undergoing restoration or repair by craftsmen who combine modern technology with traditional shipbuilding techniques, and convert ships into effigies of old-time sailing ships for use in films and TV.

Tall ships in Gloucester Docks during filming of *Alice Through the Looking Glass*.

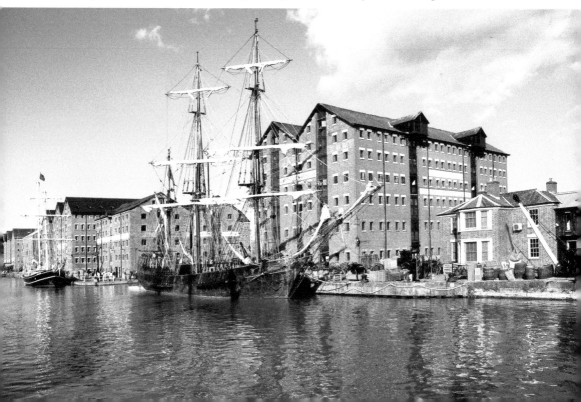

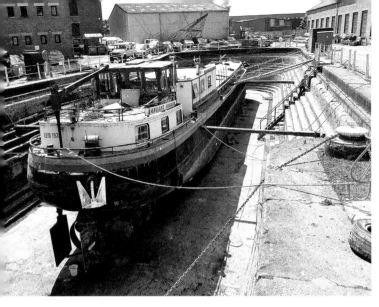

One of Gloucester's dry docks.

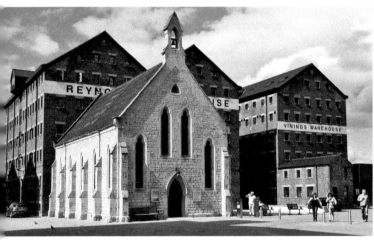

The Mariners Church and Reynolds Warehouse at Gloucester Docks.

In the centre of the docks is the Mariners Church. Due to the close proximity of a warehouse behind the church, the chancel is at the west end instead of the more usual east. The chapel was built primarily for workers at the docks and crews of visiting vessels. All seamen were welcomed and, when appropriate, the chaplain organised services in foreign languages; in its first five years 2,000 copies of the Bible and over 14,000 leaflets in twelve different languages were distributed. In the nineteenth century the chaplain also ministered to British emigrants sailing from the docks to North America.

At the north end of the Victoria Basin is the Soldiers of Gloucestershire Museum. This occupies the docks' former Custom House and tells the story of the Gloucestershire Regiment and the Gloucestershire Hussars over the last 300 years.

Impossible to miss near the regimental museum is a 21-metre-high sculpture designed by Nottingham-based artist Wolfgang Buttress. Engraved around the base are lines from the poem 'Requiem' by Gloucester's First World War poet Ivor Gurney. The sculpture's title is *The Candle*, although it is often referred to unkindly as the 'Rusty Needle'.

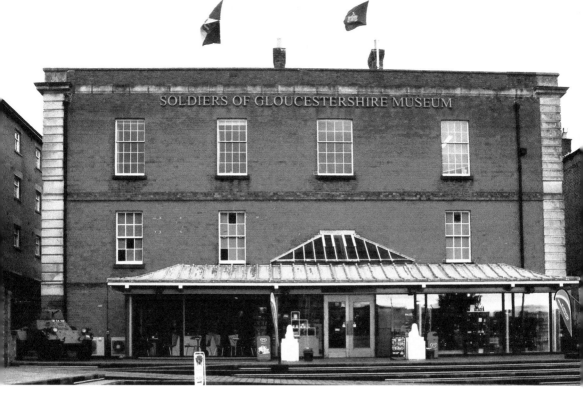

Above: The Soldiers of Gloucestershire Museum at Gloucester Docks.

Right: *The Candle* sculpture at Gloucester Docks, often irreverently called the 'Rusty Needle'.

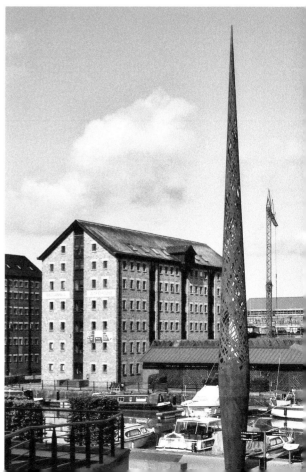

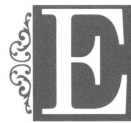

Eastgate Market

At the entrance to Eastgate Shopping Centre in Eastgate Street is an imposing entrance with tall classical columns and portico. This used to be the entrance to the city's Eastgate Market. The original entrance used to be nearer The Cross, but as part of a large redevelopment of the city centre in the 1960s the original Eastgate Market was demolished and replaced by a new shopping centre that incorporated a new market hall. However, the city council insisted that the new shopping centre should retain the original market entrance, so the old portico was dismantled and re-erected further down Eastgate Street to where it now stands.

Eastgate Market evolved from numerous speciality markets dispersed at various sites throughout the city. Gloucester's earliest known market building was the King's Board,

Classical columns and portico at the entrance to Eastgate Market.

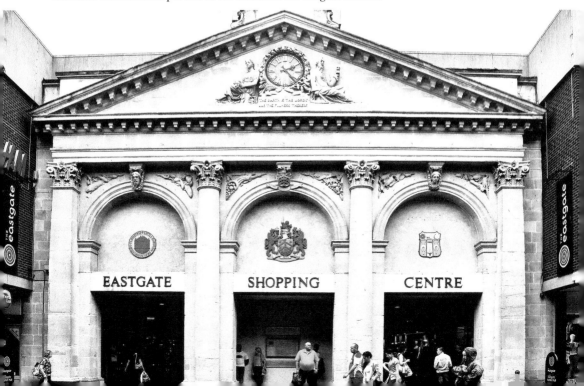

which was used for the sale of cheese and can now be seen in Hillfield Gardens off London Road. In the mid-thirteenth century a corn market was held in Westgate Street and fish was sold from carts, first near St Nicholas' Church and then in Southgate Street.

In the mid-1780s a major reorganisation of the markets took produce markets out of the streets and the old market houses were demolished. They were replaced by two new markets, one in Southgate Street and the Eastgate Market, which provided space for country market gardeners and tradesmen to sell their corn, meat, pigs, poultry, fruit, vegetables and other wares.

In 1855 the original Eastgate Market was rebuilt and the current portico added. It is constructed from classical stone blocks built in a monumental Italianate style with four two-storey-high columns bridged by arches. The keystones include a male and a female head and a central shield of arms, while the spandrels have low relief carvings of fish, fowl and fruit issuing from cornucopias. Above the arches is a pediment with a clock surrounded by a carved wreath, supported on a block bearing an extract from Psalm 24 'The Earth is the Lord's, and the Fullness Thereof'. To the sides are two seated figures: Father Time on the right and on the left Ceres, the Roman goddess of agriculture, grain crops, fertility and motherly relationships. Above the pediment is an arched bell turret flanked by scrolls and topped with another pediment.

Eastgate Street

In the Middle Ages Eastgate Street was the city's Jewish quarter and consequently was the least favoured of Gloucester's four main streets. However, in 1275 the Jews were expelled to Bristol at the insistence of Queen Eleanor. Originally called Jews' or Jewry Street, in 1330 it was renamed Ailesgate Street, finally becoming Eastgate Street in 1473. The name was originally used for the stretch of road between The Cross and Brunswick Road; beyond there it was called Lower Barton Street. In 1984 the whole

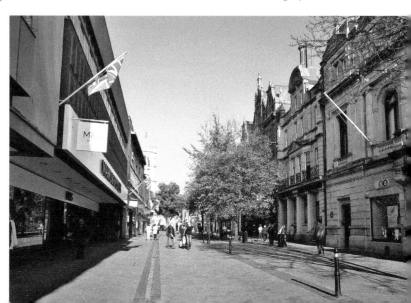

Eastgate Street looking towards The Cross.

street from The Cross to Trier Way was designated as Eastgate Street and the name Lower Barton Street disappeared.

Dominating the street next to The Cross is St Michael's Tower. Built in 1465, this is all that remains of the church of St Michael the Archangel that was demolished in 1956. The tower is now the centre for the Gloucester Civic Trust who provide guided walks through the city.

By the early twentieth century new public buildings, banks and shops had transformed the street. The most prominent group comprises the Guildhall, National Provincial (now NatWest) Bank and Lloyds Bank. This group is on the right of the accompanying photo.

Near the Guildhall the City Cinema opened in 1911, being renamed the Hippodrome in 1915. In 1955 a fire destroyed the building, but it was soon rebuilt and reopened, and then renamed the Gaumont. The cinema closed for good in 1961 and was rebuilt as British Home Stores, although that has now closed as well.

Between 1966 and 1974 the area bounded by Eastgate Street, Queen Street, Constitution Walk, Greyfriars and Southgate Street was redeveloped to create the Eastgate Shopping Centre. Bell Lane and Queen Street were incorporated as covered pedestrian ways in the new centre and a new market hall was built south of Bell Lane. A large Woolworths store was built with a frontage to both Eastgate and Southgate Streets.

Eastgate Street has also had its fair share of bars and cafés, notably the Cadena café, the Market House Inn, and Lemon and Parker's, which was one of the first pubs in Gloucester to have live music and had The Library discotheque at the back. Next to the Guildhall was the Saracens Head Hotel, which was built in 1680 and originally had a very plain exterior until it was entirely rebuilt in 1920 with an ornate cast-iron and stained-glass canopy.

Outside Boots the Chemist is a reinforced glass cabinet that provides a view of an underground chamber containing remains of the city's east gate and its defences

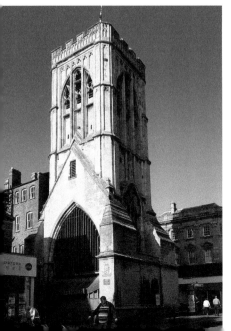

St Michael's Tower at The Cross.

dating back to Gloucester's founding as a Roman fortress in around AD 68. The site includes Roman remains, the base of a thirteenth-century tower and a Tudor 'horse-pool' where wagons and livestock were washed before market. Around the corner in Brunswick Road on the outside wall of Boots is a bas-relief sculpture depicting scenes from the Romans' occupation of Gloucester.

Near the end of Eastgate Street just before it meets Trier Way is the city's original public baths. They have been incorporated into the GL1 Leisure Centre, while the original building is now Liquid nightclub.

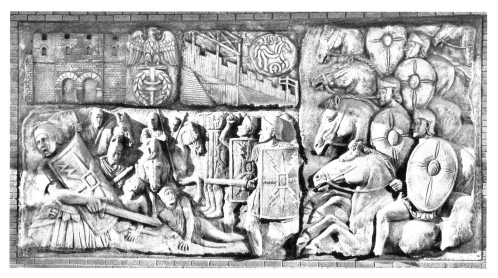

Above: Scenes from the Romans' occupation of Gloucester outside Boots the Chemist.

Below: The original public baths, now Liquid nightclub.

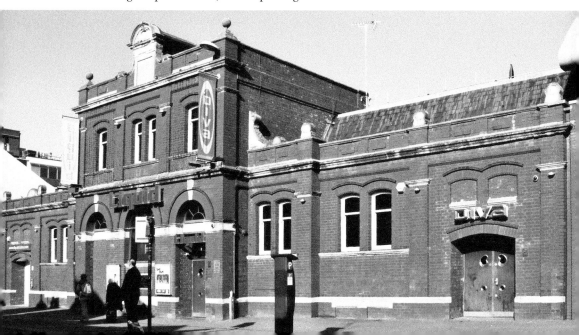

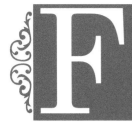

F

Fleece Hotel

The Fleece Hotel was one of three major inns in Gloucester that provided lodgings for pilgrims visiting the tomb of Edward II in the cathedral. The hotel dates from 1497 and is Grade I listed. It has been closed for some years awaiting restoration.

When viewed from Westgate Street its size is deceiving as the hotel complex includes a salt loft, Edwardian block and a great inn, as well as some adjacent properties in Westgate Street; the salt loft was formed by converting a group of cottages fronting Bull Lane.

Over a period of 300 years the hotel gradually expanded, with much of the expansion taking place during the twentieth century when the hotel extended from Westgate Street to include properties in Bull Lane and Mercer's Entry.

Beneath the hotel is a twelfth-century tunnel-vaulted undercroft that is the surviving part of a merchant's house. It is an exceptionally fine and early surviving example

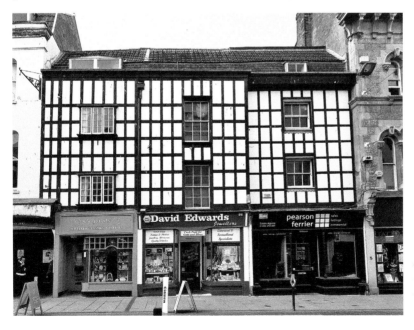

The former Fleece Hotel in Westgate Street.

of its type, and bears comparison with examples elsewhere in Britain and northern Europe. A brick walled passage leads from the north-west corner of the undercroft to a brick vaulted cellar below No. 19A Westgate Street. Before the Fleece closed the undercroft housed a lively and much-loved bar that for many years was known as the Monk's Retreat, and latterly The Bierkeller.

Fountain Inn

Tucked away down a narrow passage between Nos 51 and 53 Westgate Street is The Fountain Inn. This is one of the oldest sites connected with the brewing trade in Gloucester. Brewing was first recorded here in the early fourteenth century and continued through to the 1950s. The earliest record of The Fountain being a hostelry was in 1455.

Above the main entrance door from the courtyard is a pediment framing a block carved in bas-relief showing William III mounted on a horse with the inscription 'GVLIELMVS III'. This plaque commemorates a visit by the king, who allegedly rode his horse from the courtyard to an upstairs room to show his contempt for Jacobite rebels meeting there.

At one time it was owned by the bishop who crowned the young Henry III at St Peter's Abbey (now the cathedral) in 1216. The inn was converted into a coffee house and tavern in 1672, at the same time being named The Fountain after Trinity Well, a water source located nearby in Westgate Street.

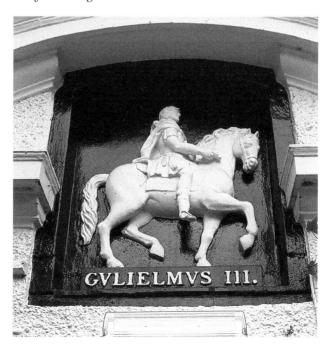

Ancient plaque commemorating William III at the Fountain Inn.

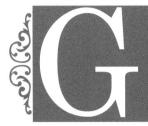

Gaudy Green

Opposite Christ Church in Brunswick Road is Brunswick Square, which is Gloucester's only remaining Georgian garden. This is not a public garden, but is mutually owned by the residents of the square and was first established in 1825.

After the Gloucester & Sharpness Canal and Gloucester Docks opened, the city was linked with the Severn Estuary and the open seas beyond and was open for shipping traffic from around the world. With the canal came 'new money' people and a new breed of business entrepreneur. By 1825 gentlemen's houses were built around the newly fashionable areas of Brunswick Square, Spa Road and Montpellier. The majority were bought by business people including mill and barge owners, metal and other merchants, clergy, and importers and exporters. Many of the owners held title to parcels of land within the square's central area, so decided to turn it into a formal

Preparing to re-enact the siege of Gloucester in Brunswick Square.

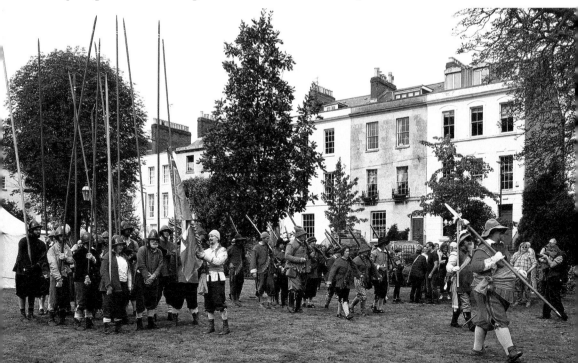

park and gardens that were to be maintained for the exclusive benefit and enjoyment of the owners and nearby residents, and a deed of covenant was drawn up stating that nothing could ever be built on the land. The managing group formed to administer the maintenance of the gardens is still in existence.

The square has played a major role in the history of the city, and its roots can be traced back to Roman times. The area on which it stands was originally known as Gaudy Green, from the Latin 'Gaudium' meaning 'to enjoy'. Being outside the city walls, the area was used for relaxation and pleasure. In 1820 Gaudy Green was renamed Brunswick Square after Caroline of Brunswick, the wife of George IV.

During the English Civil War Gloucester was a Parliamentarian city and occupied a key position at the principal river crossing into Wales. Strategically, the Royalists needed to break down the city's Parliamentarian support and control. In 1643 the king's troops led by Prince Rupert established a battery and army camp on Gaudy Green and laid siege to the city, with three huge cannons firing at the city's south gate. Both residents and the Parliamentarian army were laid up for many weeks within the walls with little food and water, but the siege held, thus changing the course of British history.

Greyfriars

Greyfriars was originally a thirteenth-century Franciscan monastery. The surviving remains are the nave and north aisle of the church and three walls of the friary and are Grade I listed. They are of particular interest as the only example in the country

Remains of Greyfriars Franciscan monastery.

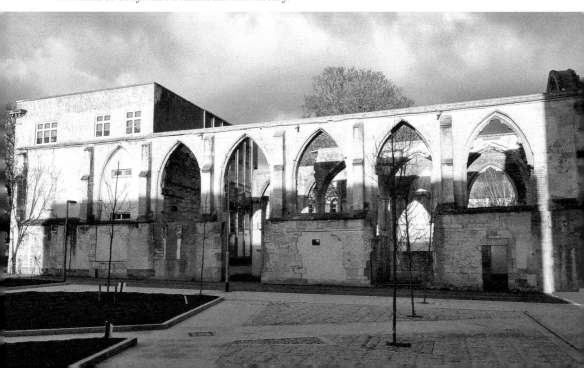

of a nave and north aisle that are of almost equal height and width. At the east end the chancel arch still stands with its moulded arch and responds intact, while below and between the large windows is some stone blind panelling that originally covered most of the church's interior wall surface. The only surviving element of the choir is the start of its north wall and the jamb of a window. On the south wall of the nave are modern replicas of stone shields bearing the arms of Chandos and Clifford of Frampton.

The friary was founded in 1231 when Thomas I of Berkeley gave the friars a site near the south gate and Henry III granted the friars the right to use timber from the Forest of Dean for its construction. The friars had their lodgings and conventual buildings on a site in Brunswick Road known as Friars' Orchard, which later became the location for the city's technical college.

After the Dissolution of the Monasteries in 1535 the friary was surrendered to the king, and then in 1542 the nave and the north aisle of the church were turned into a brewery. During the siege of Gloucester in 1643 the buildings suffered considerable damage from the Royalists' artillery. The life of the brewery was also interrupted, but despite damage to the building, the brewery reoccupied the remains until the mid-eighteenth century when it ceased to trade. The building was then subdivided into individual dwellings.

In 1810 a large house known as Suffolk House was built into the west end of the remains. That is still standing and has since been used as a dispensary, sailors' lodging house, several schools, a club for the Liberal party, and a children's library. Suffolk House can be seen at the left of the photo.

Guildhall

Gloucester's original town hall was The Tolsey at The Cross. By the late-nineteenth century increasing traffic noise from the streets was disturbing council meetings, which led the council to look for an alternative site. That was successful in 1889 when Sir Thomas Rich's School moved from Eastgate Street to new premises in Barton Street. The council identified that site as being suitable so acquired it for a new town hall, which they named the Guildhall.

The building opened in 1892 and is in a Renaissance style with carved cherubs on the upper part of the building. Offices for the town clerk, accountant, surveyor and other officials are on the ground floor, while on the first floor are the council chamber, committee rooms, mayor's parlour and public hall. The hall was used as a civic ballroom and had one of the best sprung dance floors in the county, and every year it played host to the Mayor's Ball for some of the city's children.

The building remained in use for council meetings and as the chief executive's offices until 1985 when the council moved its headquarters to a converted warehouse at the docks. The ground floor was then sold to the Cheltenham and Gloucester Building

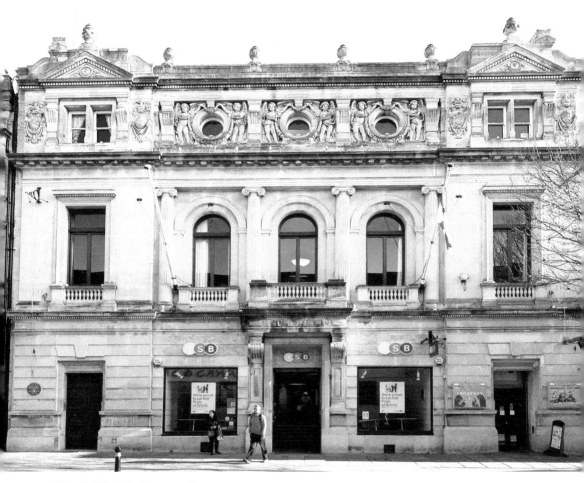

The Guildhall in Eastgate Street.

Society, and the upstairs rooms were converted into a cinema, galleries, workshops, theatre and a café-bar. The cinema is housed in the sumptuous oak-panelled former council chamber, while the theatre was originally the civic ballroom and retains its sprung floor. The staircase was remodelled in 1930 but all the principal rooms on the first floor retain their original joinery and plasterwork.

Underneath the Guildhall there are air-raid shelters, cellars and underground rooms where, it is rumoured, important documents were stored and sealed during the world wars.

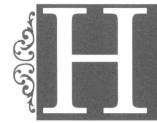

Hare Lane

Hare Lane was the original Roman road into Gloucester, joining Northgate Street a short distance outside the inner north gate. Originally called Herelone, which was an old English name for 'host' or 'army', it followed the line of the Roman road to Kingsholm and the north. Up to the late Anglo-Saxon times development of the city mainly took place around this area. In the immediate post-Norman Conquest period a gate called the Alvin Gate was erected near The Coach & Horses public house. In 1822 Worcester Street was built and replaced Hare Lane as the main entrance into the city.

Two medieval buildings give a hint of the lane's past history. Ye Olde Fish and Chippe Restaurant is housed in an early sixteenth-century merchant's house, while a short distance away is the Raven Tavern old people's centre dating from 1641. Between these outside Sainsbury's supermarket is a large bas-relief mural illustrating the history of Gloucester from Roman times to the Middle Ages. Opposite Sainsbury's is St Lucy's Garden, where the upper part of the spire removed from the nearby St John's Church is on display.

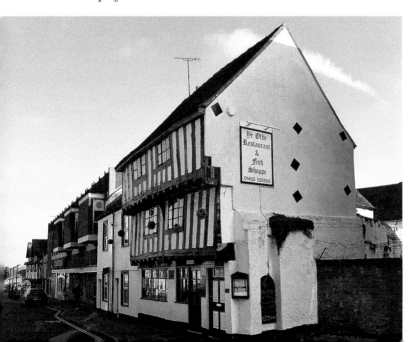

Hare Lane seen from Northgate Street.

A continuation of Hare Lane is Park Street where there is a mission room that dates from 1678. It was opened by the Society of Friends (Quakers) who purchased two cottages for use as their meeting house, and continued to use it until 1834 when they moved to a new meeting room in Greyfriars. From 1842 the Gloucester Female Mission held meetings there, supporting the work of the Gloucester City Mission that had been established to spread the gospel to the large number of poor people in the city who did not attend religious services. The mission closed its doors for the last time in October 2018.

During the twelfth and thirteenth centuries most houses in Gloucester were built with timber frames, and fires devastated large areas of the city. However, in Gouda Way, between Hare Lane and Worcester Street, are the remains of a thirteenth-century building that was built of stone, and is the reason it survives. Although it is a ruin with just parts of three walls and some fragments of doors and windows, it is important as it is the oldest non-religious building and only surviving medieval

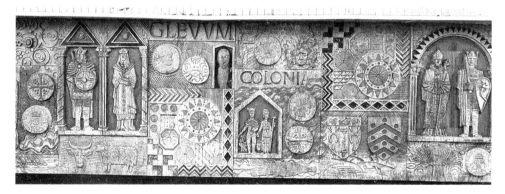

Above: Portion of mural illustrating the history of Gloucester outside Sainsbury's supermarket.

Right: Raven Tavern old people's centre.

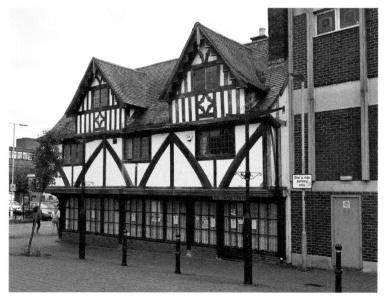

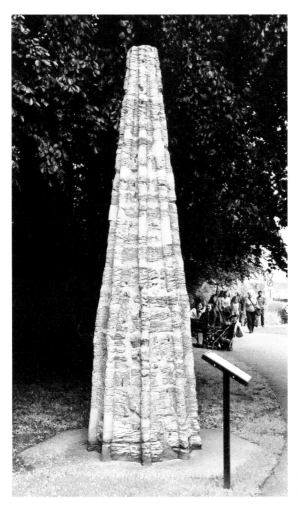

Remains of the spire of St John's
Church in St Lucy's Garden.

domestic stone house in the city. In 1540 the building was taken over by the Company
of Tanners for use as the Tanners' Hall at a time when the Hare Lane area was the
centre of the city's tanning industry, and the hall was used as a tannery until the
eighteenth century. After falling into disrepair the building almost went missing until
it was rediscovered in 1976 when Gouda Way was built. Before then it was believed
that the hall was where Sainsbury's supermarket is.

Bishop Hooper

In St Mary's Square, just outside St Mary's Gate, is a monument to Bishop John
Hooper. He was a Cistercian monk who, because of his revolutionary religious views,
fled to Europe in 1541. He eventually returned to England and was appointed Bishop
of Gloucester in 1551 during the Protestant reign of Edward VI. However, he refused

to accept the position unless he could abandon what he regarded as inappropriate details of the consecration service.

After Edward VI's death, the Duke of Northumberland tried to supplant the legitimate heiress, Mary Tudor, with his own daughter-in-law, Jane Grey. Hooper opposed this plot but when Mary became queen, Hooper, as a representative of the radical wing of Protestantism, was attacked and sent to the Fleet Prison on a charge of debt. Edward VI's legislation on the church was later repealed, but as a married man Hooper was deprived of his bishopric and kept in prison. After the heresy acts were revived in December 1554, Hooper was condemned for heresy and sent to Gloucester for execution, where on 9 February 1555 he was burned at the stake near the site of his monument.

The monument was erected by public subscription in 1857 on the site of a smaller one, and is over 10 metres high. Within the monument is a statue of Bishop Hooper standing in lengthy clerical garb. In one hand he carries a Liber Vitae book – a memorial book recording those entering into fraternity with the Church – and his other hand is held forward in greeting or benediction.

Opposite St Nicholas' Church in Westgate Street is an impressive late fifteenth-century merchant's house known as Bishop Hooper's Lodgings. It was once Hooper's home and where he spent the night before his execution. During the eighteenth and nineteenth centuries the building was used as a pin factory. Today, with its neighbours, it forms the Gloucester Life Museum, which is notable for its uneven floors, a sixteenth-century wall painting, a seventeenth-century wooden water main and a Victorian schoolroom.

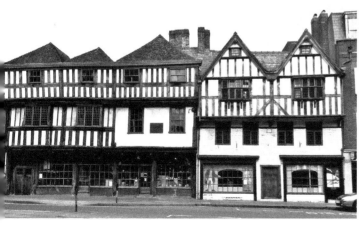

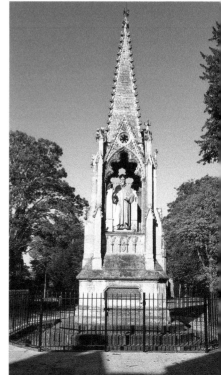

Above: Gloucester Life Museum, formerly the lodgings of Bishop Hooper.

Right: Monument to Bishop Hooper in St Mary's Square.

Imperial Inn

Although it is only a small two-storey building, what the Imperial Inn in Northgate Street lacks in size is made up for in ornamentation with an elaborately moulded and coloured glazed-tile exterior. Originally called the Plough, it has been a beer

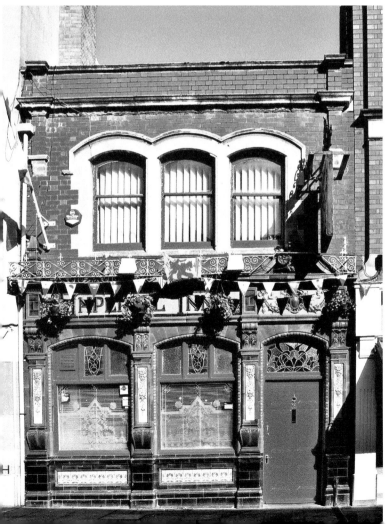

The Imperial Inn with its elaborate glazed-tile exterior.

house since 1722, although there has been a building on the site since at least 1556. It became the Imperial Inn in 1877, and the glazed-tile exterior dates from around the same time.

Infirmary Arches

These are the remains of the infirmary of St Peter's Abbey, which date from the early thirteenth century and are Grade I listed. The infirmary was originally called St Bridget's Chapel. In the seventeenth century its east end was demolished and the west end incorporated in a cluster of tenements called Babylon. In 1860 the tenements were removed, and the surviving masonry was exposed and consolidated into what is seen now.

Next to the arches is a wall marking the extent of the cathedral precincts. To the right of the wall and visible in the photograph is a house that was the birthplace of John Stafford Smith, who composed the music for the American national anthem *The Star Spangled Banner*.

The Infirmary Arches at the rear of the cathedral.

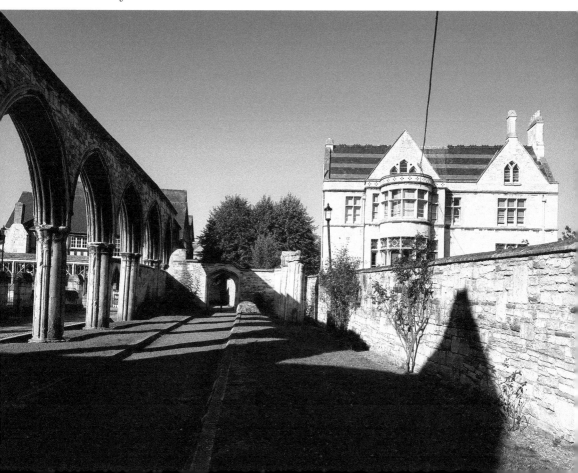

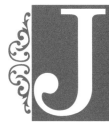

St John's Church

St John's Church in Northgate Street has been a place of worship for over a thousand years. A church said to have been founded by King Athelstan is believed to have existed here as early as AD 931. The church has the distinction of being the oldest site in the world that has been continuously used for Methodist worship, and the great evangelists John Wesley and George Whitefield both preached here.

In medieval times the church comprised a chancel, nave with a north porch and south aisle, and a tower surmounted by a spire. The aisle dates from 1234 and the tower from around 1450. In the eighteenth century the church was rebuilt. The tower and spire were retained while the rest of the church was built to a basilican plan with a classical east front and Doric columns between the nave and aisles. In the early twentieth century the top of the spire was found to be unsafe, so it was removed and rebuilt in the church's former graveyard in St John's Lane, the site of which is now known as St Lucy's Garden.

The church was originally an Anglican church called St John the Baptist. In 1972 the nearby Northgate Methodist Church was demolished and the Methodists from that church moved to St John's to share with Anglicans. At the same time the church

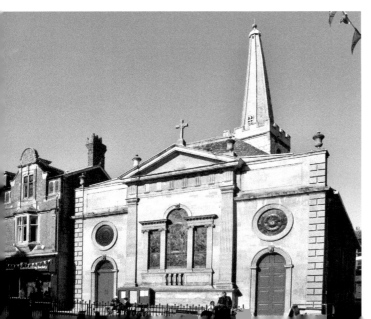

St John's Church in Northgate Street.

was renamed St John's Northgate. Since then the number of Anglican worshippers declined until in 1994 the church was formally handed over to the Methodists on a long-term lease.

St John's Lane

A short distance from The Cross down Westgate Street is St John's Lane, which is clearly identified by an ornate metal street sign bridging the lane at its entrance.

The lane dates back to the thirteenth century, and was once called Grace Lane after the long-vanished church of St Mary de Grace on the corner of Westgate Street. During the siege of Gloucester in 1643 the church was used to store ammunition. It was demolished in 1652 and the stones used for repairs to St Michael's Church at The Cross.

For many years Gloucester's daily newspaper *The Citizen* and weekly *Gloucester Journal* were printed here. The offices remain but the sound of printing presses reverberating between the walls of the narrow lane are no more. The newspapers originally had offices on both sides of the lane connected by a bridge.

Almost inevitably for a street so old, it has its own tale of a ghost. This one comes from Meek's shoe shop on the corner of Westgate Street, an Elizabethan building with a Georgian façade. On the first floor is a fine plaster ceiling dating from around 1600, where a number of people have reported hearing a spoon being stirred in a teacup when no one could be seen.

Below left: St John's Lane seen from Westgate Street.

Below right: The former offices of the *Gloucester Citizen and Journal*.

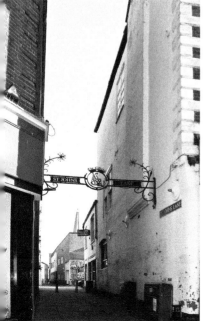
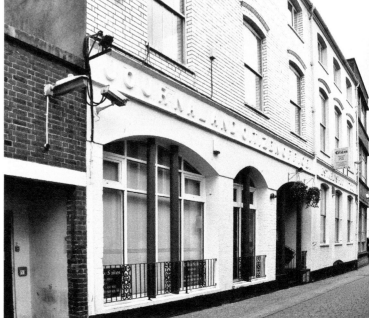

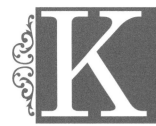

King's Board

In Hillfield Gardens, off London Road, there are two ancient monuments: Scriven's Conduit and the King's Board, which was originally erected in the late fourteenth century in Westgate Street at the end of Bull Lane. The term board is used in the sense of a table, as in the modern term board and lodging. Tradition suggests that it was a gift to the city from Richard II, though it is possible that he merely gave money to repair an existing structure.

Road improvements to Westgate Street in 1750 meant that the structure, by then an ancient monument, was an obstruction. It was dismantled and re-erected in the gardens of Marybone House on the site of Gloucester's Norman castle. In the 1780s that site was needed for a new gaol so the monument was moved to a house in Barton Street, and then in the nineteenth century it was moved again to Tibberton Court where it stayed until 1937, when it was moved to its current site.

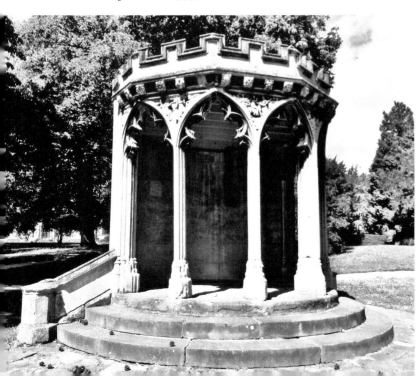

The King's Board in Hillfield Gardens.

The original purpose of the board is lost in the mists of time and is the subject of much speculation. It could have been a common preaching cross, which makes sense because the exterior is decorated with carvings depicting the life of Christ, or it could have had a more prosaic purpose such as a coin exchange. It is known that in the reign of Elizabeth I it was used as a cheese and butter market, and that in 1693 it was altered to serve as a cistern, holding water pumped from the River Severn.

Kings Square

Kings Square is Gloucester's main public open space. It was the city's main bus station until the 1960s when the central part of the city was redeveloped and the square redesigned with new shops on the east and south sides, and water fountains with stepping stones and a paddling area in the centre. By 2006 the water fountains had fallen into disrepair so the square was levelled and concreted over.

Dominating the north side of the square is the Regal public house. This was originally a cinema for which construction started in 1939, but due to the Second World War building work was halted until 1955. It finally opened as the Regal on 19 March 1956. Besides being a cinema, it was also a theatre, with stars such as Cliff Richard, Cilla Black, Roy Orbison and Morecambe and Wise performing there. The cinema closed in 1990, and then J. D. Wetherspoon took it over and converted it into a public house, keeping the original name of the Regal.

On the opposite side of the square is Gloucester's main post office. It opened in 1934 and was the city's first purpose-built head post office. At one time it was the site of

The art deco-style Regal public house.

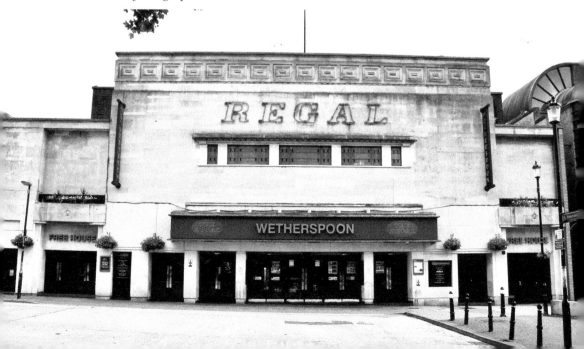

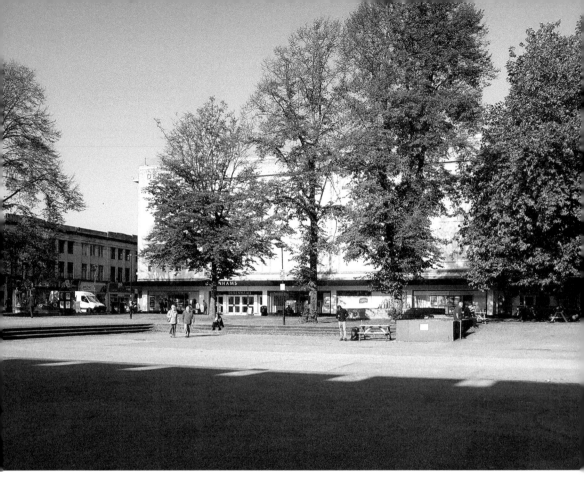

Kings Square looking towards Debenhams.

Rudhall's bell foundry, which between 1684 and 1848 produced over 5,000 bells for churches throughout Britain and North America, including the oldest peals of bells in North America at Christ Church, Boston, which were cast here in 1774.

The entire west side of the square is taken up by Debenhams department store, which also occupies all of one side of the Oxbode. The store was originally called Bon Marche, but was sold to Debenhams in 1971. During the Second World War part of the store was taken over by American forces.

Kingsholm

Long before the foundation of Gloucester as a city, Kingsholm was the site of a Roman military base. Later it was the site of an Anglo-Saxon royal palace. By the mid-eleventh century the palace was used by the kings of England, and Gloucester was a regular meeting place of the royal council.

Nowadays Kingsholm is known worldwide as the home of Gloucester Rugby, one of England's top rugby union teams. The club was formed in 1873 as Gloucester Football Club, with games being held at the Spa Cricket Ground. They are also referred to as

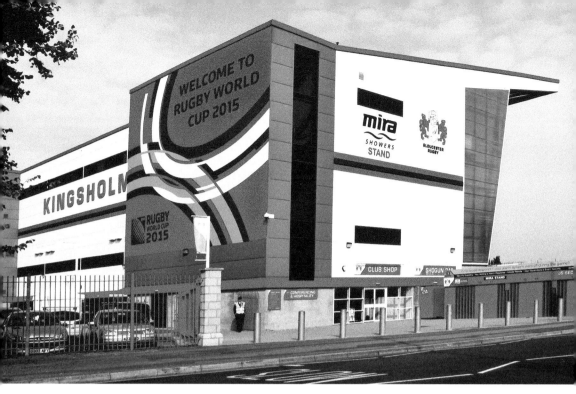

Kingsholm rugby stadium decorated for the 2015 Rugby World Cup.

the Cherry and Whites as their shirts traditionally had cherry and white hoops. In 1891 the club left the Spa and moved to its present ground, which was built on the site of a house called Castle Grim that was demolished to make way for the club. Some Gloucester rugby supporters still refer to Kingsholm as Castle Grim.

Kingsholm is well known for being one of the best rugby stadiums in England, not least for its atmosphere on match days. The most famous part of the ground is the Shed, a covered terrace running the length of the pitch that fills up well in advance of kick-off.

Gloucester won their first trophy in 1972 after beating Moseley in the inaugural National Knock-out competition at Twickenham. Success came again in 1978 when they beat Leicester Tigers in the first John Player Cup, and in 2006 and 2015 when they won the European Challenge Cup. Kingsholm stadium received worldwide attention when it hosted four matches during the 2015 Rugby World Cup.

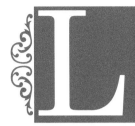

Llanthony Priory

Standing next to the Gloucester & Sharpness Canal and adjacent to Gloucestershire College are the remains of the Augustinian monastery of Llanthony Secunda Priory, the origins of which lie in the similarly named Llanthony Priory in the Black Mountains of Wales. After the death of Henry I in 1135, the Welsh priory was attacked and the canons fled to escape civil unrest and persecution. They eventually arrived here at Llanthony and became so settled that they refused to return to Wales.

Before Easter each year it was customary for a taper representing the new light of the Gospel to be lit and paraded in procession. Unfortunately, in 1301 the taper set fire to the priory's church and four bell towers were destroyed, leaving only the bare walls standing. The expense of rebuilding burdened the priory with financial problems and by the start of the 1340s the priory was heavily in debt. Much of the priory was rebuilt in the early 1500s and its finances were restored to such an extent that it became the most prosperous Augustinian house in England.

Substantial parts of the priory including part of its church survived until the siege of Gloucester in 1643. A tower that could have been used by an enemy force to overlook the city was pulled down before the siege, while other buildings were damaged during the siege as the city's defenders retaliated against Royalist artillery sited here. After the

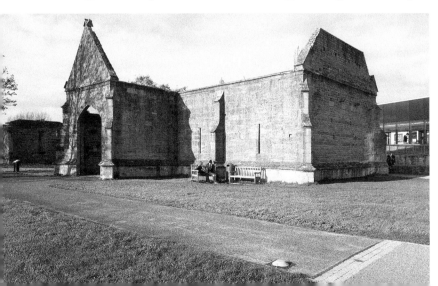

Grade I listed tithe barn at Llanthony Priory.

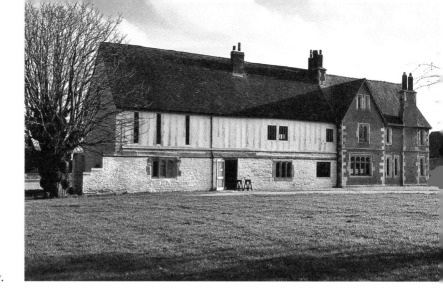

The medieval range and Victorian farmhouse at Llanthony Priory.

Civil War the priory was never used. By the start of the eighteenth century there was little left of the church, and most of the priory's buildings had been destroyed. The only significant remains are the south and west gates and the ruins of a tithe barn.

The elaborate building in the centre of the site comprises a medieval range and a Victorian farmhouse. The range was built in the fourteenth century as a single-storey limestone building, and the timber-framed upper storey was added in the fifteenth century. The adjacent farmhouse was built around 1870 on the site of a previous farmhouse and a medieval gate passage between the priory's inner and outer courts. By the 1920s it was known as Llanthony Abbey Farm.

The whole site is a Scheduled Ancient Monument and parts of it are Grade I listed including the range, the remains of the tithe barn and outer gatehouse, the precinct wall south of the outer gatehouse, and the remains of the precinct wall north of the inner gatehouse.

Longsmith Street

In the Middle Ages an important source of income for the city was from the iron trade. This was mostly based around what is now Longsmith Street, and one of its original names was Old Smithestrette, which inevitably was named after the many smiths and metalworkers who were based there. All trace of the metal trade has now disappeared. At one time there was a school on the corner of Bull Lane, and the street was then called Schoolhouse Lane.

The street is significant for a number of outstanding buildings, many of which are listed. A few metres from Southgate Street is the Black & White Restaurant, which is housed in a fine sixteenth-century timber-framed building.

A few metres further is Ladybellegate House, an eighteenth-century town house containing fine Rococo plasterwork and a carved oak staircase. It has been restored by Gloucester Civic Trust and is Grade I listed. Robert Raikes, the founder of the Sunday school movement, was born here in 1732.

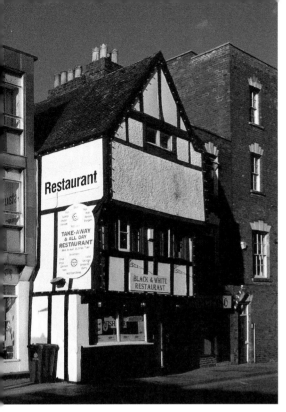

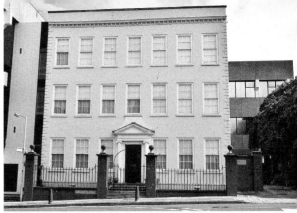

Above: Grade I listed Ladybellegate House in Longsmith Street.

Left: Sixteenth-century Black & White Restaurant in Longsmith Street.

Nearly opposite Ladybellegate House is Bearland Lodge, another eighteenth-century town house. This has an interesting pediment sculpted in high relief above the façade. In the centre is the figure of Perseus in a billowing cloak and wearing a helmet. He is sitting on the back of a lion with a winged cherub to his right, a staff in his left hand and in his right hand a shield reflecting the head of the Medusa. The pediment with its sculpture seems out of place with the façade of this small house and it is thought that it probably came from Ladybellegate House, where a similar pediment is depicted in an illustration dated 1712.

Next door to Bearland Lodge is Bearland House, which was built in the 1740s by William Jones, a distinguished Gloucester attorney. Fronting the forecourt is a restored eighteenth-century wrought-iron railing with central double gates framed by decorative flanking panels and an overthrow. From 1904 to 1909 the building housed the High School for Girls. In 1912 the west wing was demolished and replaced by a fire station that lasted until 1956. The fire station later became a transport museum, housing a number of vintage vehicles connected with the city, but has now closed. Opposite Bearland Lodge is a nine-sided building that dates from 1816. This is Gloucester's crown courts and forms part of the Shire Hall complex in Westgate Street.

This part of Longsmith Street is known as Bearland, so-called because Gloucester Castle was behind where Bearland House is now. The area around it had to be left as open space – or bare land – so that any attack on the castle could be seen. Bearland was also traditionally a site of common dunghills from at least 1372, and was still used for that purpose in 1631.

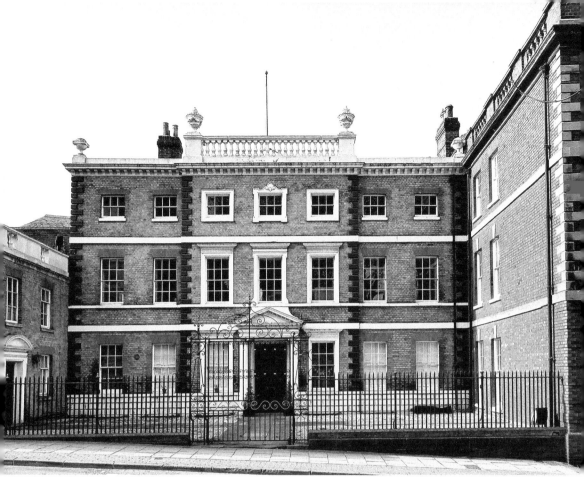

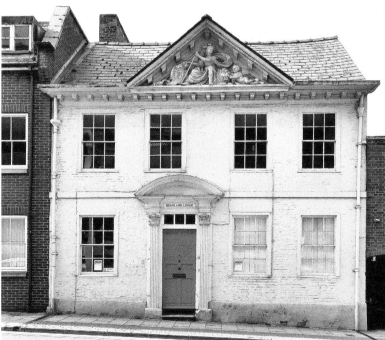

Above: Bearland House in Longsmith Street.

Right: Bearland Lodge in Longsmith Street. Note the ornate pediment.

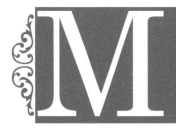

St Margaret's Hospital

In Gloucester during the early Middle Ages the disease of leprosy was rife, and a leper hospital was founded in London Road. This was named after St Margaret and St Sepulchre. Nearby there was another leper hospital for women dedicated to St Mary Magdalen. As the number of leprosy cases declined so did the need for a leper hospital, and in 1518 the hospital became St Margaret's almshouse. One hundred years later the plague became rampant, so in 1638 a pest house was built at St Margaret's to accommodate plague victims.

In 1836 St Margaret's and St Mary Magdalen's, together with St Bartholomew's in Westgate Street and St Kyneburgh's in Southgate Street, were placed under the

Chapel of St Margaret's Hospital in London Road.

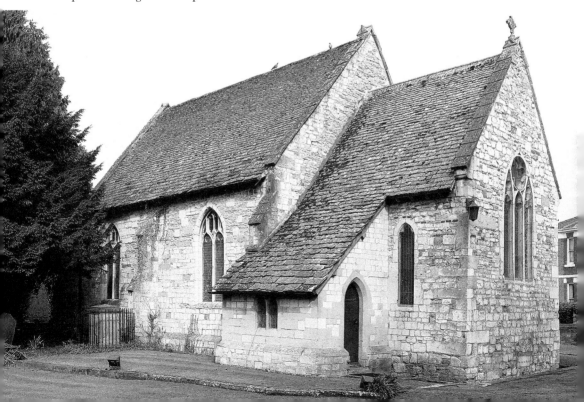

management of the Gloucester Municipal Charity trustees. St Margaret's and St Mary Magdalen's were amalgamated in 1861 as the United Hospitals, and then in 1862 St Kyneburgh's was demolished while St Margaret's was demolished and replaced by a new building. The new building included two quadrangles, one occupied by the United Hospitals' almspeople and the other by the previous residents of St Kyneburgh's.

Tucked away in a corner at the entrance to St Margaret's is a small chapel that was built in 1150. It was originally the church for St Margaret's and St Sepulchre's Hospital, although the only remains of the hospital is some twelfth-century masonry in the chapel's west wall.

St Mary de Crypt Church

On the left-hand side of Southgate Street, around 150 metres from The Cross, is the Grade I listed St Mary de Crypt Church. A church has been here since the twelfth century when it was known as St Mary in the South; the only fragment of that church to survive is a moulding above the west doorway. In the mid-sixteenth century a crypt was added, giving rise to its change of name; the crypt was formed from a space below

St Mary de Crypt Church in Southgate Street.

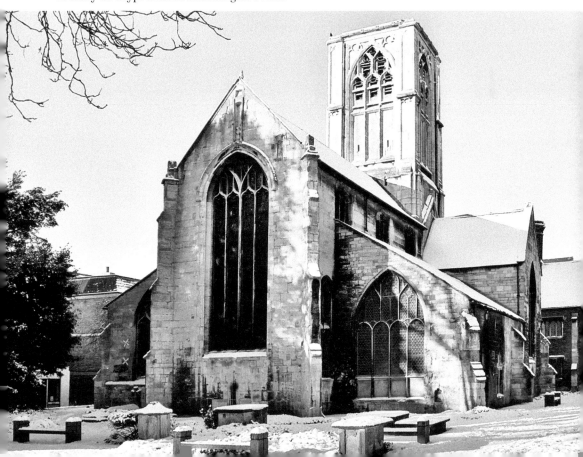

the west end of the church. In the sixteenth century the crypt housed a tavern, but that had closed by the mid-1670s. During the siege of Gloucester in 1643 the church was used as an ammunition factory and store. A number of restorations took place in the eighteenth and early nineteenth centuries, including removing battlements and pinnacles from the tower.

Many famous Gloucester people are associated with the church, including John Biddle, who was the father of English Unitarianism and a master of the adjacent Crypt School from 1641 to 1645, and George Whitefield, who was an evangelist and one of the founders of Methodism. Whitefield preached his first sermon here in 1736, and the wooden pulpit where he preached that sermon can still be seen. He then took Methodism to America from where it eventually spread worldwide. Other famous sons buried here are Robert Raikes, the founder of the Sunday school movement, and the Gloucester banker James 'Jemmy' Wood, who became famous for his penny-pinching and miserly ways.

Conjoined to the church and with an entrance in Marylone is one of England's few remaining Tudor schoolrooms. This was Crypt School, which opened in 1539. The lower floor was the schoolroom, while an upper chamber was for the master. The school crest and Gloucester's pre-Elizabethan coat of arms adorn the bay window of the master's chamber and can be seen in Southgate Street.

St Mary Magdalene's Chapel

Standing on an elevated position in London Road is St Mary Magdalene's Chapel. This is all that remains of a hospital that was established specifically to treat women with leprosy. The main part of the hospital was around 40 metres away on the opposite

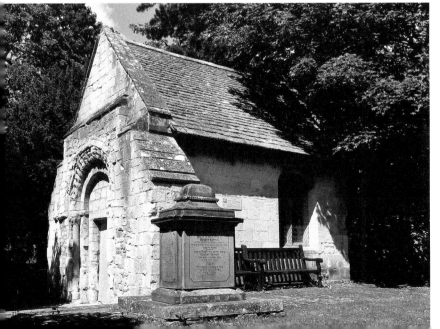

St Mary Magdalene's Chapel in London Road.

side of what is now London Road. London Road originally passed through a cutting north of the chapel, but was rerouted through the hospital grounds in the 1800s. The hospital was demolished in 1861.

The chapel contains the chancel and sanctuary of the original church, although both the chapel and its interior have been greatly altered. Within the chapel is a thirteenth-century stone effigy of a woman that is believed to be St Kyneburgh, a Saxon princess who died around AD 680 and is commemorated by Kyneburgh Tower in Southgate Street.

To the left of the entrance doorway are a number of interesting carved symbols. St Mary Magdalene was a very popular saint and a patron of lepers, so the symbols may have been the work of pilgrims who made pilgrimages here in the Middle Ages. Among the symbols are the emblems of All Saints Day, the Feast of the Holy Cross, the Star of Epiphany, the interlacing knot for the Feast of St Valentine and the fleur-de-lis of the Virgin Mary.

In 1612 James I granted funds to run the hospital and decreed that it should be known as the hospital of King James. Unfortunately for the king, the original name stuck and the hospital continued to be known as St Mary Magdalen.

St Mary's Square

Outside the cathedral precincts through St Mary's Gate is St Mary's Square. Immediately opposite the gate is a monument to Bishop Hooper at the spot where he was executed by burning at the stake. Beyond the monument is St Mary de Lode, Gloucester's oldest church.

St Mary de Lode is Grade I listed and dates from the twelfth century. The word lode comes from a nearby crossing of the River Severn, 'lode' meaning 'watercourse' in late

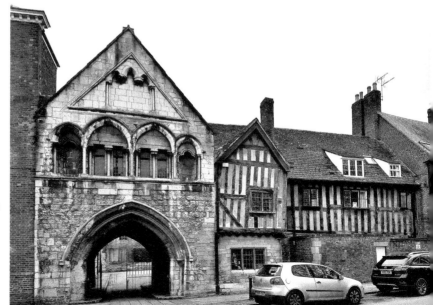

St Mary's Gate and the Almoner's Lodging seen from St Mary's Square.

Middle English. In the Middle Ages the church was usually called St Mary before the Abbey Gate. There may have been a timber church here from the sixth century, and a mainly timber nave had been built in the late ninth or tenth century. The present tower and chancel were constructed in 1190. Under a trapdoor in the nave are the remains of a large Roman building in the form of a monochrome mosaic. Extensive repairs including reconstruction of the chancel took place in 1576, while a spire above the tower was blown down by a violent storm in 1703.

The church has a carved wooden pulpit that dates from the fifteenth century and an eighteenth-century organ that was brought from the nearby St Nicholas' Church in 1972. There are also six old bells: three dating from 1705, two from 1636 and one from 1710. The most notable monument in the church is an effigy of a priest set in a defaced early fourteenth-century tomb recess on the north wall of the chancel.

During the Civil War the church was twice used to hold prisoners of war: in 1643 for Royalist troops taken at Highnam and in 1646 for those captured at Stow-on-the-Wold.

Along one side of the square is St Mary's Street, which runs into Three Cocks Lane. Hidden away behind an apartment block where these meet is an ancient statue of Charles II. Although the statue is well worn, it is still vaguely recognisable as Charles II, with his long hair to the sides and coronet on top. The statue was carved

Below left: Bishop Hooper's monument and St Mary de Lode Church in St Mary's Square.

Below right: Statue of Charles II in St Mary's Street.

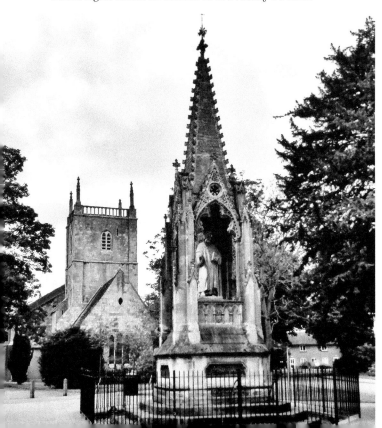
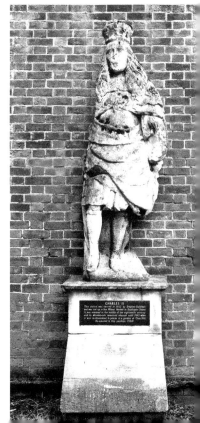

in 1662 and was originally in Southgate Street but was lost for nearly 300 years until it was found and set up in its current position in 1960. The sculptor of this statue also made a similar statue of Charles II for Worcester, and that can still be seen outside Worcester Guildhall.

Maverdine Passage

Between Nos 24 and 26 Westgate Street is a dark, narrow alley called Maverdine Passage. Because it is so narrow, unless you knew what it contained you would not give it a second look. However, it conceals a Grade I listed medieval merchant's house with a Georgian frontage that is reputed to be the finest example in Britain of a timber-framed town house. It is known as the Old Judge's House.

Dating back to the late-fifteenth century, it was once the hall of the Grocer's Guild and the mansion house of a mayor of Gloucester. In the early nineteenth century the house was the lodgings for assize judges, and then from 1886 it was occupied by Winfields seed merchants.

If you look up you can see overhanging sixteenth-century windows supported by ornately carved scroll brackets. Also visible are builders marks used in the construction of the building. Inside the building, joists on the upper floor can be seen.

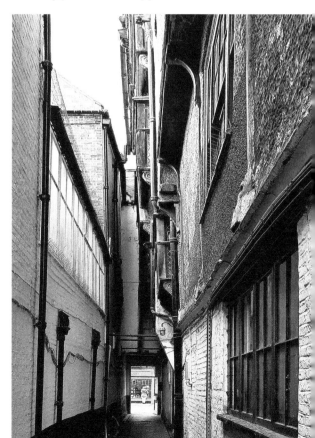

Maverdine Passage in Westgate Street.

They appear to have been made offsite as, just like an IKEA flat-pack, they each have numbers that correlate with positions in the beams into which they fit.

Unusually, the building is largely at right-angles to Westgate Street. At the upper level four phases of the original building are visible. Gables were added to the mid-sixteenth-century front bays when three bays in the centre were built in 1600, which connected to a rear stair turret and an outward extension to the passage. A first-floor door to the stair turret suggests that prior to 1600 a gallery connected the front and back ranges. The interior of the building still contains fittings from throughout its long history, while in the cellar a rubble wall is believed to contain reused Roman masonry.

There is a story that the building has the ghost of a monk who is rumoured to have murdered a woman and a slim, young man with short dark hair. The monk is always carrying a book and has been seen many times in a shed at the back of the premises.

Millers Green

Hidden away at the west end of College Green through an archway adjacent to St Mary's Gate is a well-preserved medieval close known as Millers Green; in the

The deanery in Millers Green.

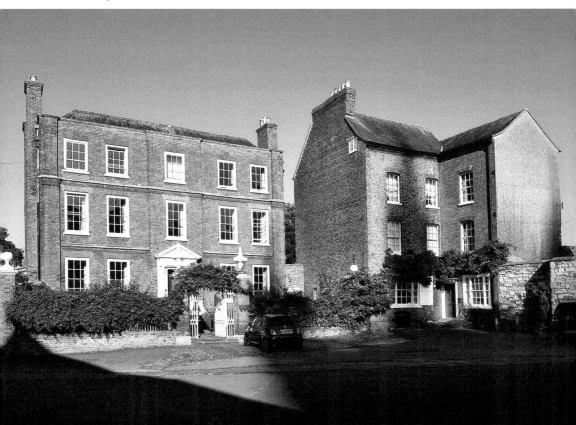

nineteenth century it was called Palace Yard. Entering Millers Green from College Green, the first house on the left was built before 1741 and is now the cathedral's deanery. Its neighbour was built around 1700 and incorporates part of a watermill used in the Middle Ages by the cathedral's predecessor, St Peter's Abbey.

No. 3 dates from the twelfth century and incorporates the remains of the great kitchen of St Peter's Abbey, although by the sixteenth century it was known as the common kitchen before being altered to a dwelling house.

Until the late nineteenth century No. 4A was the schoolmaster's house for the adjacent King's School. It was built in 1616 as the northern part of a late fourteenth or fifteenth-century monastic building, the southern half of which was remodelled to become No. 4B, a house for the King's School usher. In the nineteenth century No. 4B became the Cemetery Hotel public house. Its ground floor windows still have etched and cut lower panes with the words 'Crown Ales' and 'Cemetery Hotel'.

No. 5 dates from the sixteenth century and was originally a stable and then a washhouse but is now a small house, while No. 6 dates from the seventeenth century and is divided into three flats.

The most noteworthy building in the close is No. 7. This is the Parliament Room, so-called because it stands on a thirteenth-century stone undercroft that is the site of a building where Richard II held a parliament in 1378. Access to the Parliament Room is from College Green.

The Parliament seen from Millers Green with the cathedral behind.

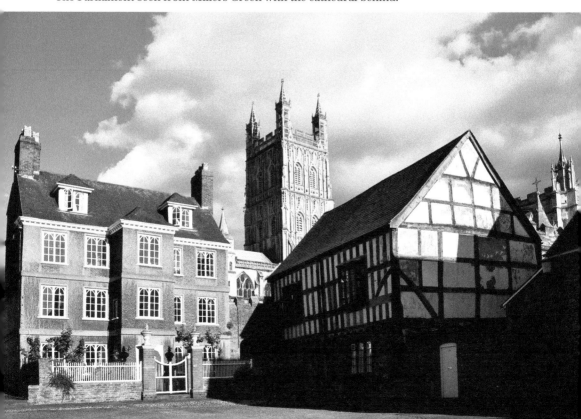

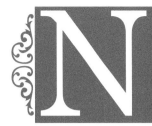

Nerva

Gloucester was founded as a Roman colony in AD 97, and was named Colonia Nerviana Glevensis in honour of the Roman emperor Marcus Cocceius Nerva.

Excavations at the Bell Inn in Southgate Street in 1969 found a statue of a Roman soldier on a horse. As only Roman emperors were depicted on horses, it was reasonably assumed that it was a statue of Nerva. A millennium project was then established to fund a statue of Nerva to mark the 1,900th anniversary of the founding of Gloucester as a Roman town. The statue was unveiled in 2002, and buried underneath is a time capsule with 130 items, including a shirt signed by the ex-Gloucester and England rugby player Phil Vickery.

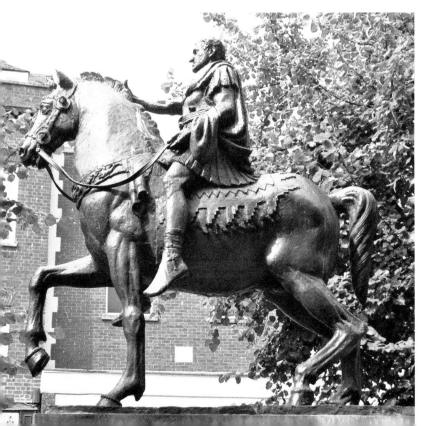

Statue of the Roman Emperor Nerva in Southgate Street.

New Inn

Just 50 metres from The Cross in Northgate Street is the New Inn, a Grade I listed building and the most complete surviving example of a medieval courtyard inn with galleries in Britain. Built between 1430 and 1450 on the site of an earlier inn, hence the seemingly inappropriate name of the New Inn, it was built for pilgrims to the tomb of Edward II in St Peter's Abbey (now Gloucester Cathedral). Close to the inn's entrance is New Inn Lane, which appropriately was originally called Pilgrims Lane. The inn remained in the abbey's possession until the Dissolution of the Monasteries in 1539. It then became a private inn, and at one time was the largest in the country. Although still a hotel and inn, there are now fewer bars than in its heyday; in the mid-twentieth century it had thirteen separate bars.

In 1553 Lady Jane Grey was staying at the inn when Edward VI died. In an attempt to keep the English throne in Protestant hands, the seventeen-year-old Lady Jane Grey was persuaded to become queen. The announcement of her succession was made from the inn's gallery, one of only three places in the country where her succession to the throne was publicly proclaimed. Adjacent to the inn's entrance is Grey's Coffee House, a reminder of that declaration, and there is also a memorial plaque outside the

The New Inn in Northgate Street.

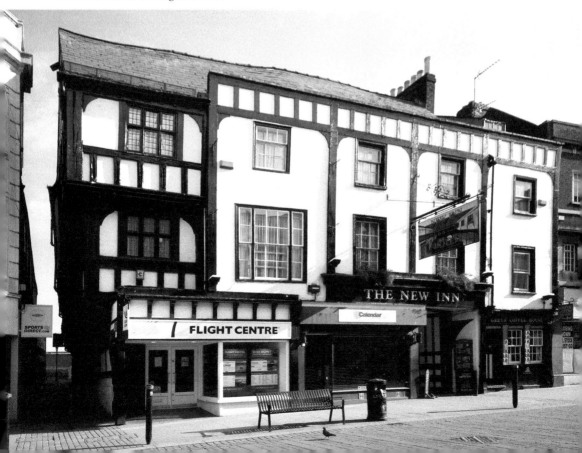

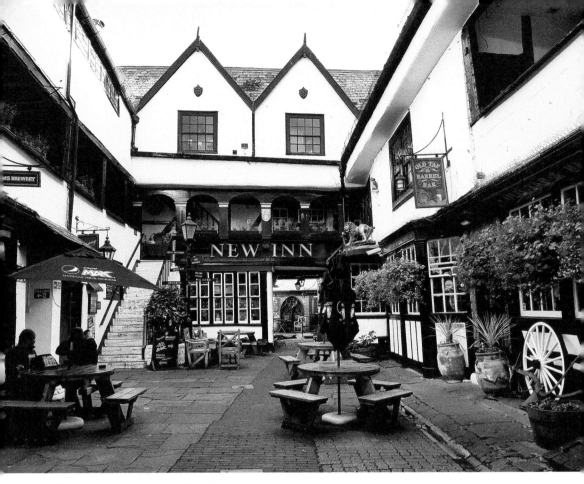

The galleried courtyard of the New Inn.

coffee house. Sadly, Jane's reign only lasted seventeen days before she was deposed by Mary Tudor and her supporters.

In the sixteenth century plays were performed in the courtyard, with audiences viewing the performances from the galleries; it is speculated that a group associated with Shakespeare may have performed here. By the eighteenth century the inn was an important staging post on the Gloucester to South Wales stagecoach route.

St Nicholas' Church

St Nicholas' Church in Westgate Street was built in the twelfth century for merchant traders. As a result it became one of Gloucester's most prosperous parish churches. The church was rebuilt in the thirteenth century and larger windows were added later. It is Grade I listed and is noteworthy for its leaning, truncated white stone spire. That was originally twice the height it is now, but during the siege of Gloucester in 1643 the spire suffered a direct hit from Royalist troops; it is now topped with an attractive coronet.

Many of the church's monuments and memorial slabs commemorate significant Gloucester citizens, some showing figures in glorious Stuart costume. On either side

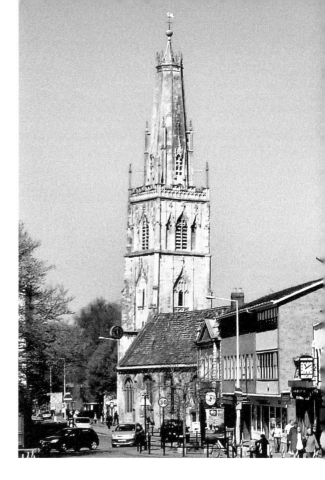

St Nicholas' Church in Westgate Street.

of the chancel are sixteenth-century squints that gave the congregation a view of the sanctuary. Above the south doorway is an unusual royal arms that references not one but three monarchs: George I, George II and Charles II.

The church is now deconsecrated and is used for concerts, talks and exhibitions.

Northgate Street

For 2,000 years the route between London and South Wales was through Gloucester, with all traffic travelling up Northgate Street, turning right at The Cross, then leaving down Westgate Street. The reason that traffic came up Northgate Street instead of via Eastgate Street stems from when the Roman Ermin Street entered the city at Kingsholm, which effectively made Northgate Street the road from London.

After the Romans left, development of Northgate Street was partly a result of planning during the late Anglo-Saxon period and partly due to the location of the gates in the Norman city wall. The north gate was immediately before St Aldate Street near the junction of Northgate Street and Hare Lane, and for a long time it was used as the city prison until a new one was built in 1786.

Since the Middle Ages the street has been a shopping street. On the western side near The Cross was the Cordwainery, a cordwainer being a maker of luxury shoes, whereas a maker of ordinary shoes was simply called a cobbler. A market house for the sale of meal was built in 1569 next to St John's Church, and until 1741 there was a pig market in upper Northgate Street.

Britain had a financial crisis in 1825, which saw many country and provincial banks fail. In response, the Bank of England opened a number of branches around the country, the first of which was opened in Gloucester at Nos 13–15 Northgate Street, which closed down in 1849.

Until the early twentieth century the street remained relatively unchanged. In 1889 John Rowe Pope purchased a small drapery and tailor's shop at No. 19. He added neighbouring properties in 1909 and 1914, purchased an adjacent store in 1929, and extended the building until it eventually became the Bon Marche, Gloucester's largest department store. The Bon Marche was sold to Debenhams in 1971. If you look up at the front of the building you will see that there are three distinct parts: the 1914 build is the part nearest St Aldate Street, while the 1909 part joins a larger building opened in 1931.

The oldest building in the street is the New Inn, one of Gloucester's greatest gems. It was built in the fifteenth century as a hostelry for St Peter's Abbey on the site of an earlier fourteenth-century inn.

Northgate Street with The Imperial and Abbey inns.

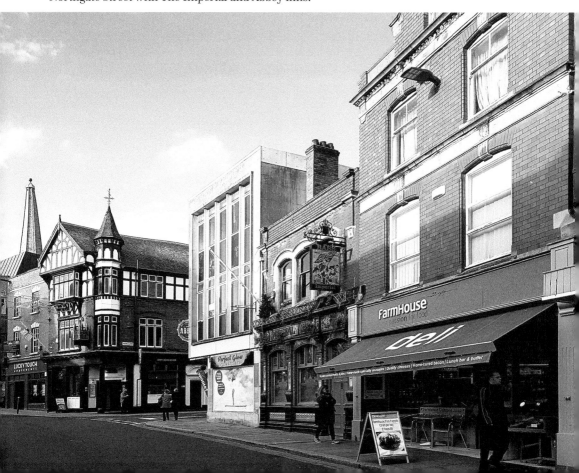

O

Old Bell Inn

Standing out among its nondescript neighbours, No. 9 Southgate Street is remarkable for the outstanding architectural quality of its carved and panelled timber façade. The building was built in 1664 as a merchant's house for Thomas Yate, an apothecary and former mayor of Gloucester; the façade dates from the same time. A mosaic set in the pavement in Southgate Street is a tribute to Yates the apothecary.

In the eighteenth century Thomas Whitefield purchased both the apothecary and Yates' home next door and converted them into the Bell Hotel. On the ground floor there were stables and stores, while the apothecary part of the building was converted into a tavern with a theatre and a ballroom for large social events. In 1785 the inn was the official stop for the coach to London.

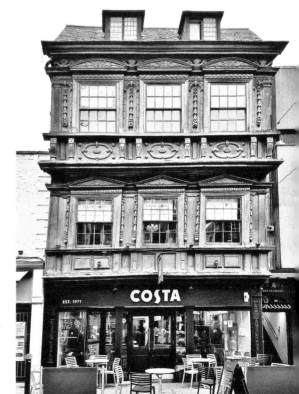

Ornate façade of the Old Bell Inn above Costa Coffee in Southgate Street.

The hotel closed in 1967 and most of it was demolished in the 1970s to make room for the Eastgate Shopping Centre. The remaining part of the hotel was converted into a Costa Coffee branch on the ground floor and the Tiger's Eye Restaurant and Old Bell Inn on the first floor. In the bar of the Old Bell is a highly decorative fireplace dating from 1650, which bears the coat of arms of the Yates family. It is unusual in that it appears to be constructed from wood but is actually made from stone, and has carvings of two lions and four cherubs, each representing Yates' four sons. Interestingly, one of the cherubs has six fingers.

Over the years, the hotel has also been known as the Old Blue Shop, so named as it was where blue dye was manufactured, and the City Tea Warehouse when it was adorned with a metal canister on the roof.

Old Crown Inn

During the siege of Gloucester in 1643 an inn called the Crown on the corner of Upper Quay Street and Westgate Street was the centre of operations for the Roundheads' leader, Colonel Edward Massey. The Crown dated back to at least 1455, although by 1680 it had become the Old Crown. It ceased trading in 1760 and all that remains of the original inn is the building known as Hyett House two doors away at No. 91 Westgate Street.

The buildings that now make up the Old Crown were originally two buildings: one of Victorian origin, while its neighbour with an ornate brick façade dates from the early to mid-eighteenth century. For many years the buildings were home to Woods Army & Navy Stores. Later it was acquired by Samuel Smiths Brewery and after extensive restoration it was re-established as a public house in 1990.

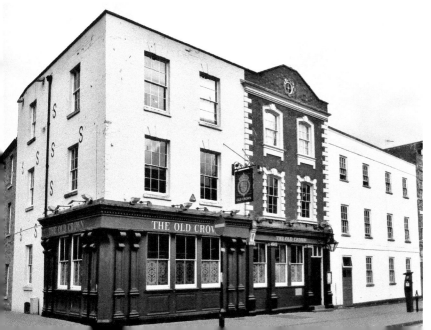

The Old Crown Inn in Westgate Street.

Oxbode

The Oxbode was originally a very narrow lane bearing no resemblance to the road of today. It was a street of slums where people could shake hands with their neighbours from the top floors of their houses. The street dates from 1263 and at one time was named Ox Body Lane. An ancient ditty whose origins are unknown makes reference to both that name and the lane's narrowness:

> There's an ox lying dead at the end of the lane
> his head on the pathway, his feet in the drain.
> The lane is so narrow his back is so wide,
> he got stuck in the road, twixt a house on each side.
>
> He couldn't go forward, he couldn't go back
> he was stuck just as tight as a nail in a crack.
> And the people all shouted 'so tightly he fits,
> we must kill him and carve him and move him in bits'.
>
> So a butcher dispatched him and then had a sale,
> of his ribs and his sirloin, his rump and his tail.
> And the farmer he told me 'I'll never again
> drive cattle to market down Ox Body Lane'.

For a time in the nineteenth century it was called Mitre Street, after a Mitre Inn that was located around halfway along what is now Debenhams. The original lane was widened in 1929, and a mosaic in the pavement at the Northgate Street end recalls its original narrowness.

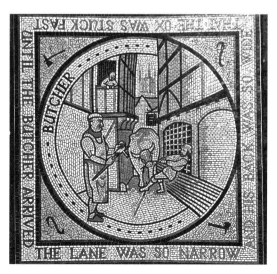

Pavement mosaic in Northgate Street at the entrance to The Oxbode.

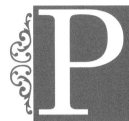

Parliament Room

Almost hidden away at the north-west corner of College Green is Church House. This is a block of three buildings that was built in the twelfth century and was originally the lodgings for the abbot of St Peter's Abbey. From 1325 it was the prior's lodging, but in 1541 when the abbey became Gloucester Cathedral after the Dissolution of the Monasteries it became the deanery.

The Parliament Room occupies the left-hand part of the block. The name comes from 1378 when Richard II held a parliament in the abbey and part of the Parliament Room was used for sittings of the commons; Henry IV continued to hold parliaments there until 1406. The northern side of the Parliament Room faces Millers Green.

The building is built above an undercroft that incorporates thirteenth-century masonry walls from an earlier hall on the site. It is remarkable for its timber-framed first floor that dates from the fifteenth century. This was originally longer than now, but was reduced to its present length in 1649. It ceased to be occupied as part of the deanery in 1720, and by the 1760s it was called the club room and was used for social gatherings.

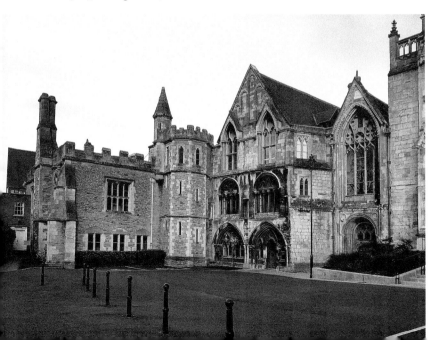

The Chapter House containing the Parliament.

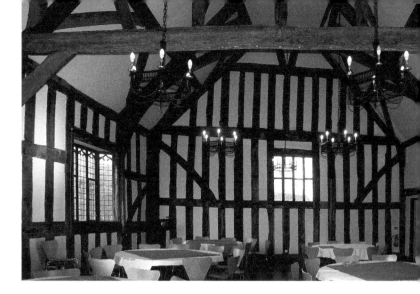

Interior of one of the
Parliament Rooms.

Pinch Belly Alley

In medieval times there were many small passageways off of Westgate Street. One of
those still there is opposite St John's Lane, and many walk past without noticing it.
This is now called Mercers' Entry but used to be called Pinch Belly Alley, and is the last
remaining tenth-century side street still in public use in the city. It was named Pinch
Belly Alley as it had stones in the walls that were positioned to stop cattle escaping
from the butchers' quarter into Westgate Street's upmarket merchants. The stones
and the old medieval wall are still visible. Previous names for the alley have also been
Love Alley and Fox Entry.

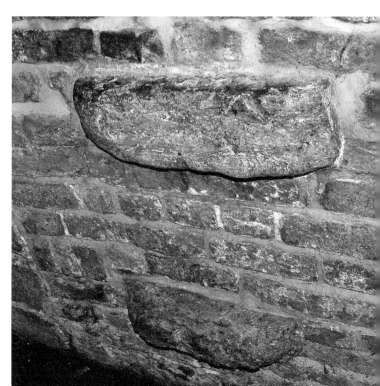

Protruding stone blocks in
Mercer's Entry, formerly
Pinch Belly Alley.

Pitt Street

Pitt Street runs from opposite the back entrance of Sainsbury's supermarket in Hare Lane to near St Oswald's Priory. The name comes from a family called Pitt who owned Paddock House. In 1780 John Pitt, the owner of the house, laid out a deer park and ornamental pond on land between there and St Catherine Street. That house and land is now part of the King's School and its playing field.

Most buildings in the street are connected with either the cathedral or the school and have remained largely unaltered for 200 years. The exception is a Gothic-style building on the corner of Park Street, which was built in 1858 and used to be Gloucester's Court of Probate. On the front is a stone panel with an inscription in raised Gothic lettering: 'Gloucester Court of Probate MDCCCVIII'.

The wall on the south side of the street was originally the precinct wall of St Peter's Abbey and also formed part of Gloucester's thirteenth-century town defences. In the sixteenth century the wall was raised and windows inserted to form part of the abbot's lodging, subsequently becoming the bishop's palace. In 1860 the palace was demolished and a new one constructed. In 1954 that became part of the King's School and a new palace called Bishopscourt was built opposite the probate office.

The Probate office in Pitt Street.

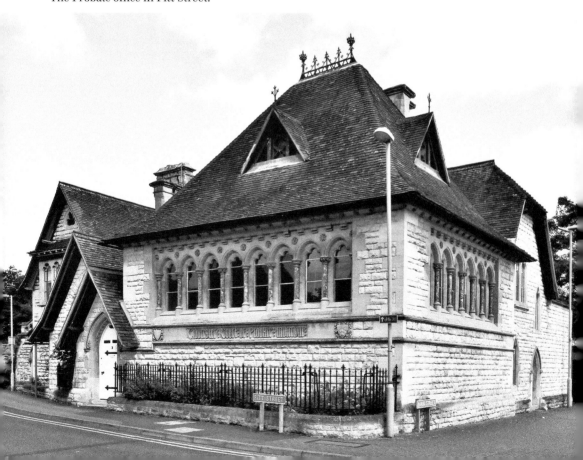

Q

Quays

Where once there was the incessant noise from machines in a large factory manufacturing giant hydraulic presses, there is now the measured calm and bustle of the Gloucester Quays outlet centre, which has a mix of high street and designer shops.

From 1866 to 2003 this was the site of Fielding & Platt's Atlas Works, one of Gloucester's largest engineering companies. In 1902 it produced Britain's first vacuum cleaner and in 1963 an aluminium plate stretcher that helped to build Concorde. After the factory closed the site lay dormant until May 2007 when it was redeveloped. Unwanted buildings were demolished, although a former furniture factory was left intact and is now part of the centre.

Main entrance to Gloucester Quays outlet centre in St Ann Way.

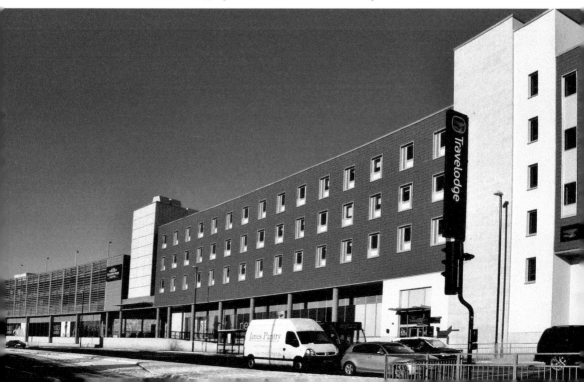

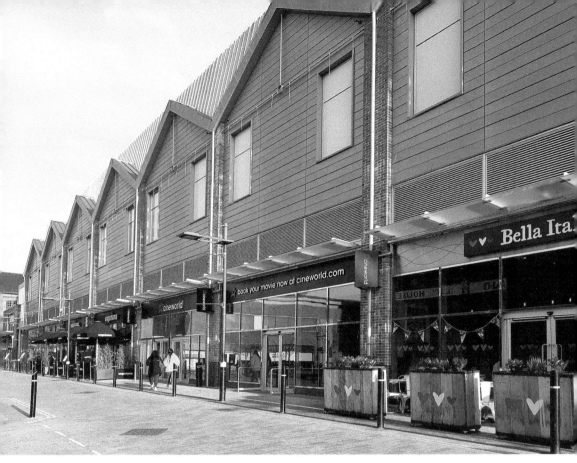

Some of the restaurants and the cinema at Gloucester Quays outlet centre.

Set in a stunning waterside location, the centre hosts regular food festivals and a ten-day Victorian Christmas market, each of which attract over 100,000 visitors. It is also very much a leisure quarter, with two hotels, a ten-screen cinema and over twenty cafés, restaurants and bars. Situated next to the complex is the National Waterways Museum and historic Gloucester Docks, where tall ships are often to be seen.

R

Raikes, Robert

Robert Raikes was the founder of the Sunday school movement and one of Gloucester's most famous sons. His name is perpetuated in the public house at Nos 36–38 Southgate Street named the Robert Raikes House, a magnificent timber-framed merchant's house dating from 1560.

Raikes was born in 1736 and educated at the Crypt School opposite Robert Raikes House. He inherited the *Gloucester Journal* newspaper from his father, and through this medium he became instrumental in spreading the Sunday school movement throughout the world. He moved the *Gloucester Journal* into this building in 1758, and then in 1772 moved here with his family.

The building subsequently became a shop, restaurant, and the Dirty Duck and Golden Cross public houses. After an exceptional restoration the building reopened as the Robert Raikes House public house in November 2008.

In Gloucester Park there is a bronze statue of Raikes standing on a tall plinth with his head down holding an open book. It was erected where there was once a cannon captured during the Crimean War. This statue is a replica of similar ones in Victoria Embankment Gardens in London and Toronto in Canada.

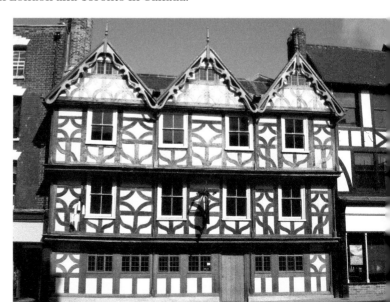

Robert Raikes House in Southgate Street.

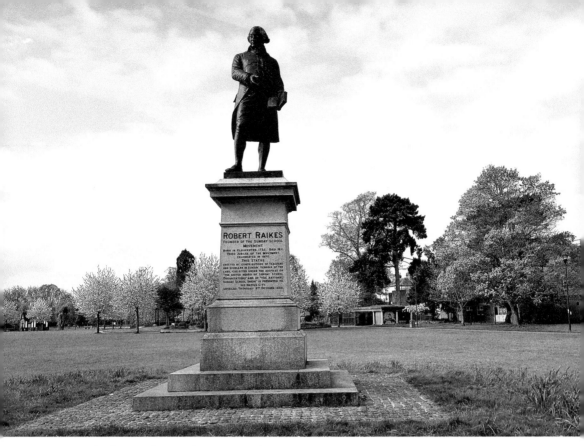

Statue of Robert Raikes in Gloucester Park.

Rudhall's Bell Foundry

Bell founding was a Gloucester industry for at least 700 years. One of the leading foundries was Rudhall's, which was started by Abraham Rudhall, who developed a method of tuning bells by turning them on a lathe rather than the traditional method of chipping with a chisel. As far as is known Abraham Rudhall's foundry was on the corner of Archdeacon Street and Westgate Street.

The foundry was notable in that the oldest bells in North America were cast there: eight bells were cast for the Old North Church in Boston, USA, and are still there in its steeple. One of the bells has the inscription: 'We are the first ring of bells cast for the British Empire in North America, A. R. 1744'. There are also five bells still hanging in Wells Cathedral that were cast by Rudhall's in 1757.

Rudhall's son was also a fully qualified bell founder. His foundry was on the site of the post office in Kings Square, a fact recorded on a blue plaque next to its entrance. In 1815 the foundry was taken over by the Whitechapel Bell Foundry in London.

Henshaw's was another bell foundry, and is believed to have given its name to Bell Lane, now Bell Walk in the Eastgate Shopping Centre. Set into the pavement in Southgate Street near to the shopping centre entrance is a mosaic that commemorates Henshaw's part in the city's bell-making history.

Scriven's Conduit

In Hillfield Gardens, off London Road, there are two ancient monuments: the King's Board and Scriven's Conduit, which was originally erected in 1636 in the middle of Southgate Street nearly opposite what is now the entrance to Eastgate Shopping Centre. It provided Gloucester with a public water supply, the water being supplied via lead pipes from Robinswood Hill. A pair of seventeenth-century well heads still survive on the hill.

Although the conduit had a practical purpose, it was also highly decorative with carved stone medallions depicting the resources of the Vale of Gloucester, and between the medallions are projecting heads of lions. It was originally topped with a statue of Jupiter Flavius, the Roman god of rain, who poured rainwater into Sabrina, goddess of the River Severn, the name 'Sabrina' being Latin for 'Severn'.

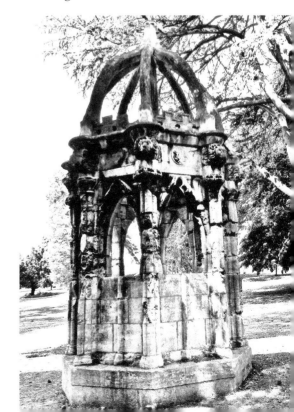

Scriven's Conduit in Hillfield Gardens.

There are also six roundels carved with allegorical scenes including a view of Gloucester from the south; Ceres, the goddess of agriculture; an unknown seated figure; Bacchus, god of wine and revelry pouring wine into a cup, and representing Gloucester's flourishing wine trade; and the River Severn with two sailing ships. The final roundel is too badly damaged to determine what it originally looked like.

The structure was dismantled in 1784 and moved to a garden in Dog Lane, where King's Walk shopping centre is now. That area was redeveloped in the 1830s and it was moved to Edgeworth Manor until 1937, when it was returned to Gloucester and re-erected in its present location.

Shire Hall

The Shire Hall in Westgate Street was built in 1816 to the design of Sir Robert Smirke, who also designed the British Museum in London. The grand entrance is said to be styled on the temple that stands on the River Ilissus in Greece. The central Ionic portico is all that remains of the original building. Substantial extensions to either side of the front entrance were made in the early twentieth century.

The building was originally built for Gloucestershire's magistrates. The front part of the building now houses the administrative headquarters of Gloucestershire County Council and at the rear are two semicircular courtrooms.

During the early 1960s the front part of the original building except for the entrance portico and flanking wings was rebuilt. The whole complex was massively enlarged with blocks of offices added on the west side, which were extended over Bearland to connect with another new block that incorporated the county police headquarters. The extension to the building stands on the site of the Booth Hall, which was Gloucester's first town hall. The old Booth Hall became the Alhambra music hall in 1869, then from 1876 it was used as a circus and skating rink, a variety theatre, and from 1907 it was the King's Hall Picture House, Gloucester's first cinema.

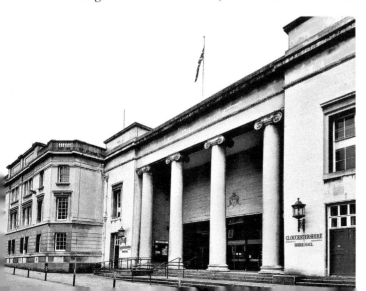

Shire Hall in Westgate Street with its Ionic portico.

Southgate Street

Southgate Street appears to be a nondescript collection of shops, but look closer and its heritage soon becomes apparent. Starting at St Michael's Tower at The Cross and looking at the buildings on the street's east side, we soon come to G. A. Baker's, jewellers. Look up and you will see the most famous clock in Gloucester.

Next door is Costa Coffee, above which is the Tiger's Eye bar and restaurant. Its façade gives a hint of its illustrious past when it was the Bell Hotel. A few metres further is a statue of the Roman Emperor Nerva on his horse, then the entrance to the Eastgate Shopping Centre that was built in the 1960s during the redevelopment of this part of the city.

A few metres further on is an archway at the entrance to a passage called Marylone. On the right of this passage is the original schoolroom of Gloucester's first grammar school, Crypt School, which was founded in 1539. The school building forms part of the adjacent medieval St Mary de Crypt Church. A short walk along Marylone is Café René, which has a medieval well in the middle of its main bar. At the far side of the church is a cobbled lane leading to the meeting house of the Society of Friends (Quakers) and the ruins of Greyfriars, a thirteenth-century Franciscan monastery.

Carrying on down Southgate Street, at the junction with Commercial Road, is Kimbrose Triangle, which is named after Kyneburgh, an Anglo-Saxon princess who wished to dedicate her life to God and ran away to Gloucester where she was murdered

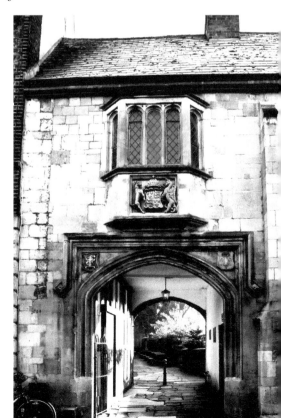

Entrance to Marylone in Southgate Street.

and thrown down a well. The well became known as St Kyneburgh's fountain and became a place of pilgrimage as it was reputed to have healing powers. The site of the well is marked by Kyneburgh Tower, a 17-metre-tall piece of public art that is symbolic of the well and is also on the general line of Gloucester's original city wall.

Next to the tower on the corner of Parliament Street is the Furniture Exhibition Centre. Inside this shop part of the city's Roman wall can be viewed. A further 200 metres brings you to the Whitesmiths Arms, parts of which date from the fifteenth century. The building is an anomaly as it was thought that all buildings outside the south gate were demolished during the siege of Gloucester in 1643. However, in 1996 it was extended into an adjacent building that was found to date back to the fifteenth century; the original fifteenth-century roof beams are clearly visible in one of the rooms.

Returning towards The Cross on the west side of the street, the triangular building at the apex of Kimbrose Triangle was built in 1849 as the Gloucester Savings Bank. Then opposite Greyfriars is a narrow lane leading to Blackfriars Priory, the most complete surviving Dominican priory in Britain. A few metres further is the New County Hotel, which was the first commercial premises in Gloucester to have a telephone. It was originally The Old Ram and with the New Inn in Northgate Street and the Fleece Hotel in Westgate Street was one of Gloucester's 'three great inns of the abbey'.

Southgate Street with Kimbrose Triangle and the former Gloucester Savings Bank.

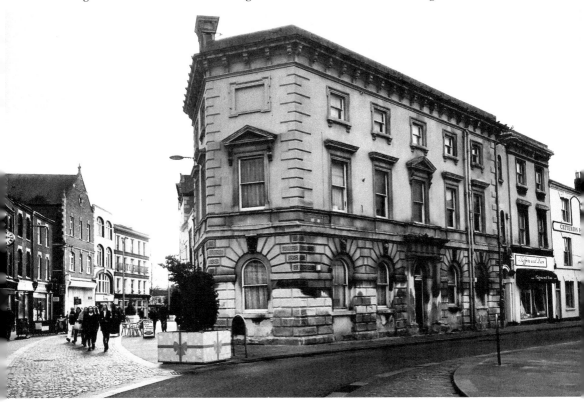

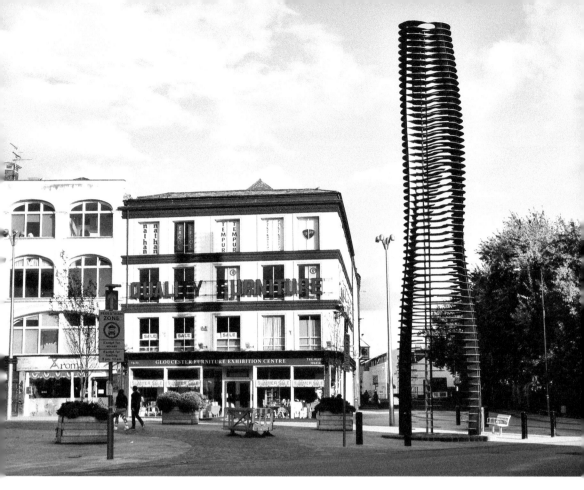

Above: St Kyneburgh's Needle in Southgate Street.

Right: Half-timbered building in Southgate Street on the corner of Longsmith Street.

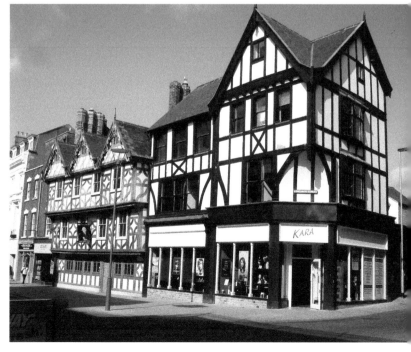

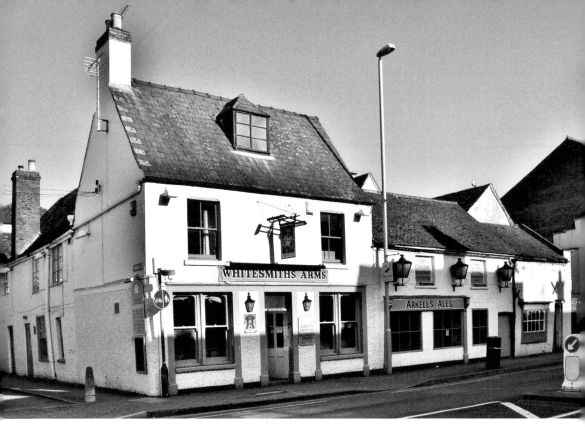

The Whitesmiths Arms in Southgate Street.

Next is the timber-framed Robert Raikes House, then on the corner of Longsmith Street is a half-timbered building that was remodelled from two older properties and designed to blend in with Robert Raikes House. The last lane before we get back to The Cross is Cross Keys Lane, which was the centre of the city's cloth trade during the tenth century.

Sword Inn

At first sight the Sword Inn in Westgate Street seems an unremarkable double-fronted building. However, look closely and you will see that the left-hand part is gabled while the right-hand part has a plain front. Walk a few metres towards The Cross and look more closely at the top storey of the right-hand building and you will see that while it matches the appearance of its neighbour, only the centre window is genuine, and the two windows flanking it are simply painted replicas for show.

The building dates from the sixteenth century but did not open as an inn until 1680, and then only in the left-hand building, which did not extend into the next door building until 1990. It was called The Sword until at least 1736, but from 1847 until 1849 and again from 1920 it was the Union Inn; between those years it was used as a wine vaults.

A tailor called John Pritchard once had his workshop in the right-hand building. One weekend he had gone home leaving a waistcoat uncompleted, but when he returned on Monday morning the waistcoat was finished. He displayed it in the window with a sign

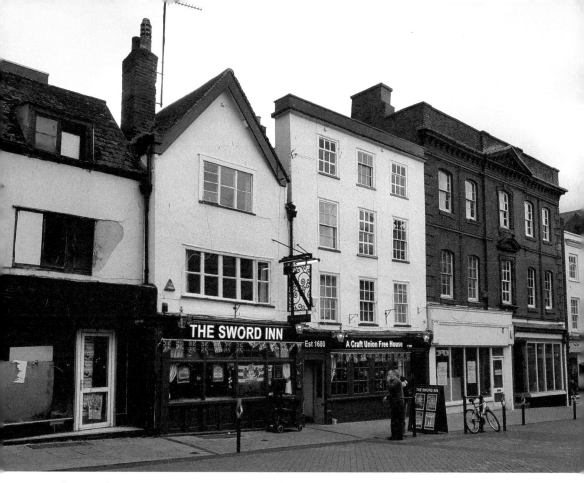

The Sword Inn in Westgate Street. Note the false top storey.

'Come to Pritchard where the waistcoats are made by the fairies'. The reality was that his staff had gone out on the Saturday night and as one of them had a key to the shop they spent the night there. To pass the time on the Sunday they decided to finish the waistcoat, but couldn't complete the last buttonhole so left a message 'No more twist'.

Beatrix Potter was visiting the Gloucester area in 1897 and heard the tale of the waistcoat that was mysteriously completed over the weekend, and used it as the basis for her story *The Tailor of Gloucester*. In 1990 the Union was extended into the building that housed Pritchard's workshop, so it was renamed The Tailor's House in recognition of the tale. The name reverted to the Union in 2003, but has now gone back to the original name of The Sword.

Three Cocks Lane

Near the bottom of Westgate Street just before St Nicholas' Church is Three Cocks Lane, an unprepossessing passage that runs into St Mary's Street. These were originally the same street called Abbey Lane, and ended at one of the medieval city gates called the Blindgate, which was approximately at the end of what is now Pitt Street.

Although the lane is unremarkable, it is noteworthy for a carving of Gloucester's coat of arms high up on a wall by the entrance from Westgate Street. At the sides of the shield is a pair of naked cherubs each seated on a heraldic beast, a lion on one side and unicorn on the other. The armorial bearings were carved in 1745 for the front of the old Booth Hall in Westgate Street, which was demolished in 1957. After restoration and regilding, the coat of arms was erected here in 1961.

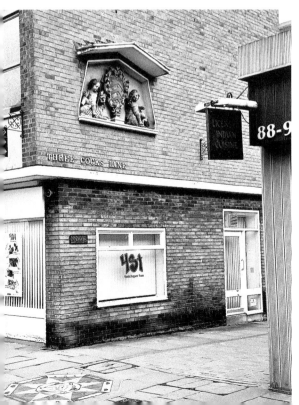

Three Cocks Lane seen from Westgate Street showing the Booth Hall pediment.

U

Upper Quay Street

Originally built in the thirteenth century as a lane leading to Gloucester's castle, Upper Quay Street is one of four streets in this area that suggest Gloucester has a history of using the River Severn for trading; the other streets are Lower Quay Street, Quay Street and The Quay. Since at least the fourteenth century and long before the construction of the Gloucester & Sharpness Canal and the docks, goods were landed at the quay and shipped out from there. Trade at the quay continued until the mid-1960s. The only building to survive as a reminder of the trade once carried on there is the old Custom House.

Upper Quay Street now runs from Westgate Street to Bearland, the only building of note being the Old Crown Inn on the corner of Westgate Street. Until 1957 the city's first town hall, the Booth Hall, was on the opposite corner, while for many years the Co-operative Society had a creamery on the corner of Bearland.

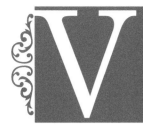

Via Sacra

The Via Sacra is a circular walk around the centre of Gloucester broadly following the line of the Roman walls. The route starts and finishes at the cathedral and is identified by black or contrasting alternating paving. Sub texts on street signs and finger posts at various points mark the route, which crosses all of the gate streets at various points and passes numerous historic landmarks.

Leave the cathedral through King Edward's Gate and College Street, turn left into Westgate Street, noting the Shire Hall just to your right, then immediately turn right into Berkeley Street and continue to Longsmith Street where you will see an eighteenth-century town house, Bearland House, facing you. To its left is Bearland

Gloucester City Museum on the Via Sacra.

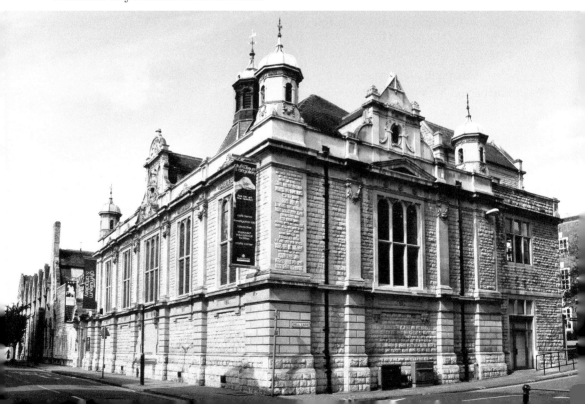

Lodge, another very attractive eighteenth-century house with an interesting pediment above the façade. Walk up Longsmith Street to Ladybellegate House on the left. Built in 1705, the interior contains some outstanding rococo-style ornamental plasterwork.

Now turn right into Ladybellegate Street then left into Blackfriars and you will see Blackfriars Priory on your right. Continue to Southgate Street and go straight across into Greyfriars past St Mary de Crypt Church and its graveyard and you will see Addison's Folly next to a side entrance to Eastgate Shopping Centre. The folly was built in 1864 in memory of Robert Raikes by local solicitor Thomas Fern Addison. Continue along Greyfriars past the ruins of the thirteenth-century Greyfriars Priory until just before Brunswick Road on the corner of Constitution Walk and you come to the City Museum and Art Gallery. Among the museum's treasures is a Celtic mirror.

Turn left into Constitution Walk, pass the rear of the museum, then continue past the back of Boots to Eastgate Street. On your right, protected by toughened glass, you can view an underground chamber containing remains of the city's defences, its east gate and some Roman remains.

Go straight across Eastgate Street into Kings Walk shopping mall and you will see three stainless steel plates set into the pavement. These lead down to the city's bastion that contains historic remains of Gloucester's Roman wall and a medieval defensive tower constructed during the reign of Henry III; the bastion is regularly open to the public.

Continue along Kings Walk to the end of Kings Square at The Chambers public house, then turn left into St Aldate Street and continue to Northgate Street where you will see St John's Church opposite. Cross over Northgate Street into St John's Lane with St John's church hall on your right, then turn right into St Lucy's Garden; this was the north-east corner of the precinct of St Peter's Abbey. The only surviving piece of the precinct's east wall can be seen in the corner of the garden behind the church hall, although a better preserved stretch of the north wall runs along Pitt Street. After 35 metres turn left along the path marked Cathedral Way/Via Sacra and a short walk will bring you back to the cathedral, ending opposite the great east window.

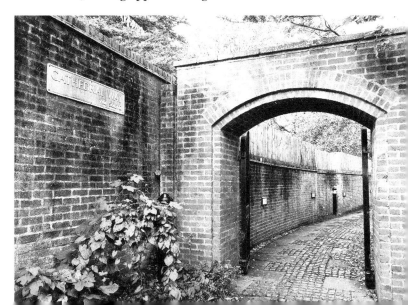

Via Sacra marked out with blocks in Cathedral Way.

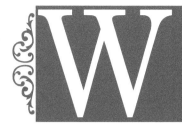

Westgate Street

For over 1,000 years Westgate Street was strategically important as it led to the lowest place on the River Severn where it could be crossed. Several of its medieval alleys and side streets still exist, and behind modern shop fronts many of the buildings are largely unchanged. In medieval times there were also buildings in the middle of the street, and though the buildings have disappeared, their locations can be seen, marked by dark-coloured bricks set into the pavement. One block of buildings was between The Cross and St John's Lane, with the street on its north side called the Mercery and that on the south side called the Butchery. Beyond here in the middle of

Westgate Street seen from The Cross.

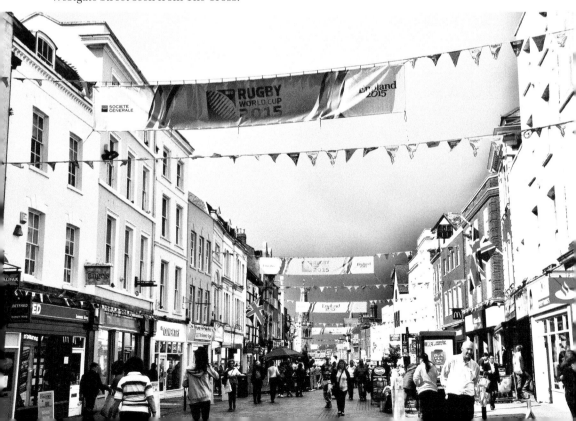

the street was the King's Board, which still exists but has been moved and is now in Hillfield Gardens in London Road.

Walking down Westgate Street from The Cross we first come to St John's Lane, marked by an ornamental name plate spanning the lane's entrance, then just past McDonald's is Maverdine Passage where, hidden away, is Britain's finest example of a timber-framed town house. In the eighteenth century the building that is now McDonald's was the Old Gloucester Bank and was owned by Jemmy 'James' Wood, at that time Britain's richest commoner.

A further 40 metres brings us to College Court, a medieval alley notable for The World of Beatrix Potter, which replicates the illustrations of the tailor's shop in Beatrix Potter's story *The Tailor of Gloucester*. In Victorian times the site now occupied by the large store on the corner of College Court was the Theatre Royal. Another 60 metres bring us to College Street, which is the main approach from Westgate Street to the cathedral.

Carrying on down Westgate Street we pass Three Cocks Lane, which leads to Bishop Hooper's monument, Dick Whittington's public house, and then come to the twelfth-century St Nicholas' Church.

Opposite St Nicholas' Church on the south side of the street are three 500-year-old timber-framed buildings that form the Gloucester Life Museum, which provides an insight to the city's social history. Four doors up Westgate Street is the sixteenth-century Hyett House with the former White Lamp Inn next door. On the corner of Upper Quay Street is the Old Crown Inn, built on the site of an inn that was the centre of operations for Colonel Edward Massey during the siege of Gloucester in 1643.

Beyond Upper Quay Street, the Shire Hall is unmistakeable with its central Ionic portico, then just past Berkeley Street is a narrow passage leading to the fifteenth-century Fountain Inn. Four doors further is The Sword Inn, which incorporates a tailor's shop that provided the inspiration for Beatrix Potter's story *The Tailor of Gloucester*. Next is Gloucester's narrowest street, Bull Lane, then opposite McDonald's is the half-timbered frontage of the former Fleece Hotel. Finally, opposite St John's Lane is the extremely narrow Mercer's Entry, which was originally called Pinch Belly Alley on account of its narrow width.

Whittington, Dick

Many people will have heard the tale of Dick Whittington, who went to London to make his fortune, but not many realise that he was a real person. When he was thirteen he was sent to London to be apprenticed to John Fitzwarren. He eventually became the greatest merchant in medieval England, and was mayor of London four times.

In the fifteenth century Dick's nephew Richard Whittington, Lord of Staunton, built the building in Westgate Street that is now Dick Whittington's public house. The magnificent brick façade was added in the eighteenth century. During the seventeenth century it was leased by John Taylor, who got into trouble for having the mayor and aldermen around while he had servants dying of the plague in the house; one of these

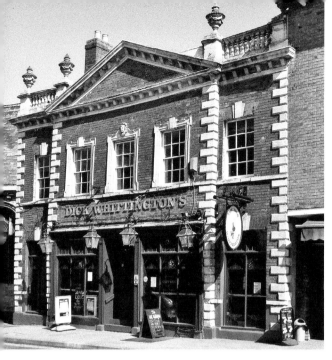

Dick Whittington's public house in Westgate Street.

is still said to haunt the pub's downstairs Black Cat bar. For a time in the nineteenth century the house was used for public worship by Protestant Dissenters. The building was completely restored in 1980 and is now Grade I listed.

Wood, James 'Jemmy'

Outside McDonald's in Westgate Street is a blue plaque dedicated to James Wood, who was usually known as Jemmy, and became nationally known as 'The Gloucester Miser'. He was a caricaturist's dream – his forehead receded at a sharp angle, his nose was well developed, and his mouth and eyes indicated a love of pleasure – and he appeared in statuettes, cartoons and toby jugs. He was thought to be the inspiration behind Charles Dickens' Scrooge, and a long-running dispute over his will is echoed in Dickens' novel *Bleak House*.

Jemmy was born in Gloucester in 1756 and inherited the Old City Bank at No. 22 Westgate Street from his grandfather. The site of that building is now McDonald's. The Old City Bank eventually became part of Lloyds Bank in 1897.

He was an untidy man, looking more a tramp than a rich banker, but had a vast personal fortune and was known as the richest commoner in His Majesty's dominions. However, he was chiefly known for his spectacular meanness, being renowned for walking everywhere rather than paying the cost of a carriage. It is said that on a journey to London a fellow traveller made fun of his ragged clothing, but Wood bet him £5 that he could withdraw £100,000 from a bank on his arrival in the city. The fellow passenger did not believe him but when Wood was able to show that he could do just that, his travelling companion was forced to hand over the £5. Wood died in 1836 worth £1.25 million, which would be worth £100 million in today's money.

X

X Marks the Spot

Rather than X, The Cross is the meeting point of the Gloucester's four main streets – Westgate, Eastgate, Northgate and Southgate streets – and has been an important meeting place throughout history dating all the way back to the Romans. The four gate streets form the arms of a cross drawn through the heart of the city and its main shopping areas spring from these roads. Lining both sides of the streets are a number of thin black bollards with their tops painted gold that represent Gloucester's history of manufacturing pins and needles.

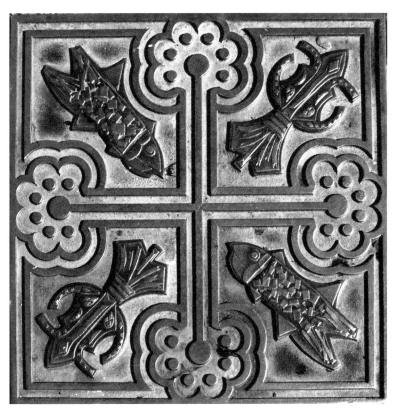

Brass plaque marking the centre of The Cross.

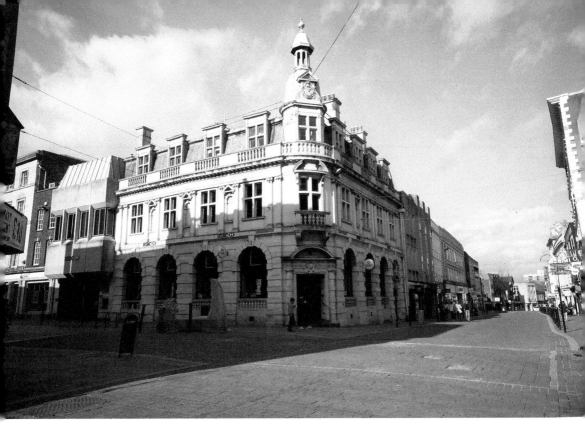

The Cross, once the crossroads of England.

Set into the pavement in the gate streets are a number of mosaics portraying trades historically associated with the city and other notable characteristics of its past. Narrative mosaics to be seen in Northgate Street are butchery, leather goods making, dying, pin making, inn keeping and tanning; Southgate Street has examples of bell founding, apothecary, market trading and tailoring; while Westgate Street mosaics show a bull, metalworking and the legal profession.

For many years The Cross was known as the crossroads of England. Before the M5 motorway and the Severn Bridge were built all traffic travelling from the north to the south-west of England and from London to South Wales had to pass through Gloucester and over The Cross. As traffic volumes increased there were inevitably problems with conflicting traffic movements, and a policeman was often on point duty doing his best to keep traffic moving. The *Daily Mail* once described the policeman on traffic duty here as the busiest in England.

Y

Yeoman Inn

Where Commercial Road meets Southgate Street is a building in a symmetrical Italianate style. It was built in 1849 and was originally known as the Black Swan Hotel. In 1970 it was renamed The Yeoman Inn in commemoration of the Royal Gloucestershire Hussars, a volunteer yeomanry regiment that became part of the British Army Reserve. The inn sign showed a Royal Gloucestershire Hussar in a tank during the Second World War. A similar building opposite was originally the Gloucester Savings Bank.

The Yeoman Inn when named the Black Swan Hotel.

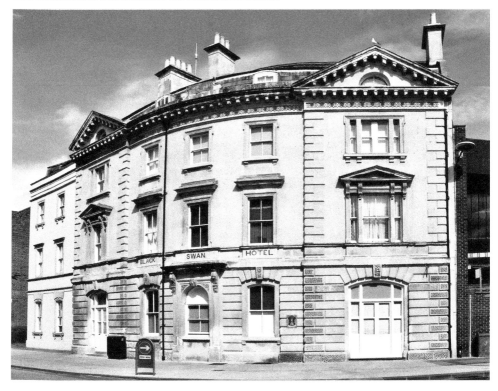

Zoons Court

If you approach Gloucester by the A417 road from the east, soon after dropping down the Cotswold escarpment you will come to the strangely named Zoons Court roundabout. The roundabout has an odd alignment as it was built as a temporary junction with the A417, part of the Brockworth bypass, the intention being to continue the new road north-westwards around the lower slopes of Churchdown Hill to Elmbridge Court roundabout. That plan never materialised and Zoons Court roundabout looks destined to remain permanent.

Zoons Court itself is an eighteenth-century farmhouse on the slopes of the nearby Churchdown Hill, although there has been a farmstead there since 1689. In the eighteenth century there was a vineyard nearby. Until the nineteenth century access was via a ford near Pitt Mill in Hucclecote, but in 1886 the owner of Zoons Court paid for a bridge to replace the ford. From 2003 to 2016 the court's coach house was the head office of the company behind the inventor Trevor Baylis's the Wind-up Radio Company, but the company has now been dissolved.

Bibliography

The following books and websites have been invaluable resources:

Fosbrook, Revd Thomas Dudley, *An Original History of the City of Gloucester*, (London, 1819)
Kirkby, Darrell, *The Story of Gloucester's Pubs* (Stroud: The History Press, 2012)

British History Online – A History of the County of Gloucester: Volume 4, the City of Gloucester.
Historic – https://historicengland.org.uk/listing/the-list/

About the Author

Roger Smith has lived in Gloucester for over sixty years, and spent most of his working life as a technical author. He is passionate about the city and its history, and has written many articles about its streets and suburbs. Roger's other interests include rugby, railways and photography. *A–Z of Gloucester* is his first book.

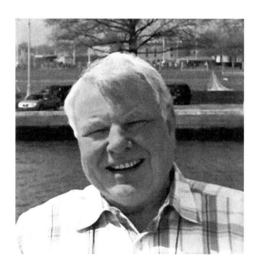